To: Opal
Best Wishes!

D1648916

"I know Rebecca Contreras to be a most effective executive leader, entrepreneur, team builder, and change agent, based on the twenty years I have worked with and remained in close contact with her. She has been nationally recognized for her many professional accomplishments and appointed to several nationally prominent, nonprofit boards. How she became so successful is a remarkable story: nothing about her youth and formal education would have predicted such success, but her wisdom, energy, faith, courage, and work ethic carried the day."

—Clay Johnson, former Assistant to the President and Director of Presidential Personnel, and Deputy Director for Management at the Office of Management and Budget (long-term mentor to Rebecca)

"Rebecca's story is every woman's story, one of failures and successes, of challenges and accomplishments, one of pain and sorrows but also of triumph and joy, one of fears and agony but also of courage and determination. Every little girl, every teen, and every woman of any background can be as inspired as I was by Rebecca's amazing trail-blazing journey."

—Rosario Marin, Former 41st U.S. Treasurer

"There are no shortcuts to true success. It takes guts, determination, wisdom, vision, and in almost every case, divine intervention. Rebecca's story is perhaps the most inspirational I have ever witnessed. As her pastor of twenty-five years, I've stood amazed as she navigated the journey from poverty and projects to political power and entrepreneurial success. There is so much insight for living your best life to be found on the pages of this book. I could not recommend it more enthusiastically."

— Rob Koke, Founder & Senior, Pastor Shoreline Church, Austin, Texas

"Rebecca's life is a true testament to God's grace and faithfulness. Her story is one of my favorites and inspires so many!"

—Rene Banglesdorf, author of *Stand Up: How to Flourish When the Odds are Stacked Against You*, CEO, Charlie Bravo Aviation

"I thank God, our Lord and Savior for bringing Rebecca into my life. From our first meeting in early 1991, I knew there was something very special about her.

From less-than humble beginnings, I watched Rebecca emerge from a cocoon-like being into a butterfly and become the beautiful person who was always there inside her. The Lord has enabled her to take risks and to develop her God-given talents to the fullest. I am so proud of being part of that development as her mentor early on and seeing her continue to succeed on the path she has taken."

—DONNA REYNOLDS, HR Director for former Texas Treasurer Kay Bailey Hutchison & Governor George W. Bush, (early career mentor to Rebecca)

"Rebecca has been a huge inspiration in my life. My mother was murdered by my stepfather when I was five, so I grew up a ward of the state. I had so much trauma in my life, I was a complete mess—a single mother of four children, on welfare, and with no true goals in life. Rebecca used her past experiences to give me hope. She mentored me and helped me see beyond my circumstances. Her powerful story and support gave me the strength to carry on and completely get off welfare. I owe Rebeca everything!!"

—MARIA HERNANDEZ, Drop Out Prevention Specialist, AISD (Rebecca mentee and key influencer through the Contreras's work with LaunchPad)

"Rebecca is the embodiment of the American dream. Her story is a testament not only to this great land of opportunity for all, but to God's redemptive power to change our lives forever. She has been an inspiration and close counsel to me for nearly two decades, and I am confident you will also benefit from her journey and the wisdom and truths she has discovered along the way."

—JODEY ARRINGTON, U.S. Congressman (former Rebecca Texas intern hire 1995; former White House PPO colleague)

"Rebecca Contreras's personal story of perseverance and faith defines the essence of bold, compassionate leadership. This autobiography powerfully captures her rise from humble beginnings to one of Texas's most inspirational entrepreneurs. It's a must-read for anyone who wants to dream big and learn how to achieve their goals."

—LESLIE SANCHEZ, author of *You've Come a Long Way, Maybe* and CBS News Political Analyst

"Rebecca Contreras is the ultimate American success story. She started out in the Welfare-to-Work Program and worked her way into the White House.

Rebecca inspires everyone she meets. She is a loyal friend and fiercely loves God, family, and her country. Her success journey is truly a message of hope and the American dream. I believe Rebecca is one of the most astute businesswomen I have ever met, and her wisdom will help others succeed. Her autobiography, *Lost Girl*, is a must-read!"

—Lisa Copeland, Chief Expansion Officer,
The Agentcy, eXp Realty, LLC, Author, Speaker

"I had the pleasure of working for Rebecca Contreras at the White House. She was one of the most focused, disciplined, and results-oriented people I have ever known. But what was even more remarkable was her attitude. Anything could be accomplished. The more I learned from her, the more I learned about her—the origins of her being. Her philosophy of life was born of her own personal life experiences. With grace and determination, she took all that the world handed her and shaped it into one of the most beautiful American stories. Her very existence represents the promise and the possibility of overcoming obstacles and challenges and making life count in every way. To a large degree, I believe she hired me because she saw just a bit of me in her. Every life she touches is made more beautiful."

—Eric L. Motley, Executive Vice President and Corporate Secretary,
The Aspen Institute, former Special Assistant to the President, The
White House (Rebecca's deputy hire in White House PPO)

"Rebecca's powerful story will resonate and inspire anyone who dares to dream big. I had the pleasure of working alongside her for nearly ten years, during both her early-on Executive Vice President consulting days as one of her senior managers in the practice and for six years with her AG company as one of her senior consultants. She only sees what's possible, and not only uses all the tools in her toolbox to get there, but she teaches you how to build your own. I've had the deep privilege of hearing about her transformative journey one-on-one, and I'm so excited for her to share it with all of you."

—Jen Tress, Senior Consultant, Public/Private
Sectors (former leader on Rebecca's team)

"I first met Rebecca in 2008 when she was Executive Vice President of another consulting firm. She gave me literally twenty minutes in between her client meetings at the USDA building in Washington DC to interview me for a new consulting role. She saw something in me that I didn't see in myself, and it started a friendship of more than thirteen years. Working with her was initially a bit intimidating with her beautiful, energetic, charismatic, and confident demeanor. She expects nothing less than perfection, pushing me to be my best. It was years later that I came to know her personal story, how she overcame the traumatic events in her life to pursue her dreams. Undeterred by not having a higher education, she learned from the ground up by capitalizing on her incredible intelligence, surrounding herself with mentors and champions, and leveraging the strengths of those around her—all leading to her amazing success."

—Karen Rarick, Current Managing Director for AvantGarde LLC and Senior Consulting Team Member to Rebecca

"Rebecca Contreras's riveting autobiography removes any excuses for staying stuck. Her transparency and willingness to be raw and vulnerable are marks of a true leader. Rebecca's story is a portrait of the power of the human spirit and evidence of the providence of God. The words in this book will plant hope in the heart of every reader."

—Jan Goss, CEO, Civility Consulting and Executive Coach to Rebecca Contreras

"If a life of bad decisions has brought you difficulties that seem too hard to overcome, then you must read my friend and former White House colleague Rebecca's book, *Lost Girl*. Rebecca's story is one of redemption and hope and demonstrates how God took her from humble beginnings to advising the President of the United States in the White House. Take it from me, going from a life of hopelessness to one of hope is worth more than all the gold in Fort Knox."

— Edmund C. Moy, 38th Director of the United States Mint (2006-2011)

From the hood to the White House to Millionaire Entrepreneur

REBECCA CONTRERAS

Published by Boss Media

Cover design by: Sara Young
Cover photo by: Nick Austin - The Celtic Viking Studio

ISBN: 978-1-954089-60-0 1 2 3 4 5 6 7 8 9 10

Printed in the United States of America

DEDICATION

I dedicate this book to my tremendously loving immediate family—my husband David, my son Caleb, my daughter Crystaline, my son-in-law Chris, my granddaughter Bella, my grandson Judah, like-my-second-daughter Elicia, and my great nephew Arrion (or as we call him, "Little man genius").

I love you all dearly!

Here's to us!

A NOTE FROM THE AUTHOR

I want to encourage and validate all those who have not given up on their dream, who have stayed the course, who have not allowed issues or challenges to take you out of the game, who have fought, reformed, changed, and pushed forward—be encouraged and stand through it all. Your dream will be realized!

CONTENTS

ACKNOWLEDGEMENTS

I want to thank God and His amazing hand of grace, mercy, and favor on my life. God is the supernatural fuel that keeps me going.

I want to thank my husband, David, who has been with me through it all—thick and thin, high and low, chaos and normal. You have been my biggest cheerleader. I was truly born to love you forever.

Thank you to my rock star children Crystal, Caleb, and Elicia for genuinely blessing me with the best gift ever—being your mom and having the opportunity to enjoy the fruits of my labor in your growth!

I want to thank Michelle, one of my good friends and my publisher for chasing me down for over ten years (literally) and encouraging me to write my story.

I want to thank my cowriter, Sherrie, who was amazing throughout the entire process of writing my story. I could never have depicted my journey in such a rich way without her.

I want to express my sincere gratitude to Donna, my very first mentor in my state government journey. She believed and invested in me when I didn't have much to offer and didn't believe in myself.

I want to thank my long-term White House boss and twenty-year-plus mentor, Clay. Never for a moment did Clay doubt my ability to get the job done. In essence, he was the reason I had access and exposure to the president so that my work could speak for itself.

Thank you to President George W. Bush for allowing me to serve you for thirteen years, first in Texas and then in your administration in DC. In my world and in the view of so many great Americans, you are one of the best presidents ever! I truly love and admire you.

I also want to thank my early youth leaders, Dave and Lupita, who saw my potential early on when I was a mess and didn't give up hope to see my life transformed, as well as my senior pastors, Rob and Laura, who have been by our side for twenty-five years at our home church of Shoreline Christian Center in Austin. I want to thank my spiritual advisor and executive coach, Jan, and my tremendous AG management team for all you do to help me be proud to lead you. Last, but certainly not least, my sincerest thanks to my Texas "chicas" (as I call them) and best friends Lisa, Rene, Cathy, and the other amazing women too many to name here (you know who you are), those that have invested in me and continue to cheer me on as success happens and do life with me. Having such precious friendships has really enriched my life.

And I want to thank two people in heaven who I can't wait to see again one day—my rock, Grandma Keta, for rescuing me and showing me grit and my mom, Grace, who never stopped praying for me or believing that one day I would be free and for raising my baby during the first year of her life. All the early pain I sustained as a child was undone in that one unbelievable act of redemption and selfless service to my daughter, Crystaline!

FOREWORD

It's not often you get a front-row seat to witness an event or a life that is so impactful and transformative, it requires you to take a step back and ask yourself, *How could this be possible? How could someone with a demolished foundation of body, mind, spirit, emotions, and environment dig out from the rubble of a grossly dysfunctional life? And not only dig out, but how could this same person rise to the levels of someone who was born into a two-parent home and guided and groomed from childhood with the best education to pursue professional careers and leadership roles in government and business? Most importantly, how did she become a well-rounded human being, wife, and mom grounded as a contributing member of society?*

As I reflect from my front-row vantage point, it's important to realize that we've all been given a free will and choices in life regardless of the cards we've been dealt—good, bad, or indifferent.

I first met Rebecca when she was nineteen, and it was clear to me her beauty was her blessing and at the same time, her curse. It was difficult to imagine the hellish lifestyle she knew as normal. I could see she was emotionally unstable, had no identity or value in her true self, and definitely had no way forward out of her "mess," as she put it. But in glimpses, I saw her work hard, demonstrating that hidden underneath was a genuine "diamond in the rough" waiting to be uncovered, reshaped, and revealed as a true gem. For a diamond to grow, it requires heat and pressure, and then once discovered, it undergoes a long strategic process to bring it into its full brilliance. Rebecca's path to where she is now was similar.

Spending time getting to know my new friend Rebecca was heartwarming, but it was also shocking to learn of her radical lifestyle and upbringing. Her wrong choices and bad behaviors prevented her from moving in the right direction, but I saw her willingness to honestly deal with her past and go deep to pursue full healing. She was in a new place, surrounded by new people, and she forced herself to cut all previous ties. Her commitment to renew herself was admirable. Knowing the pain she had experienced and then watching her firsthand in our young marriage face her guilt, shame, and low self-esteem, I recognized that hard work would be needed to break through her heart, emotions, and downright negative mindsets. Yet, every step of the way, day after day, week after week, month after month, and year after year, this young woman (then wife and mom) was willing to endure and accept the responsibilities and actions she needed to own.

How do I know she is the real deal? Well, I've been married to her now for over thirty-one years, and from my front-row seat, I've witnessed her excel. Next to my walk with God, having the privilege to parent my princess, Crystaline, and the birth of my son, it has been the best view ever. I stand in awe of her hard work, relentless drive, and tremendous accomplishments, and even more so her passion and love for people and community.

Today, she is adored by her adult children and young grandchildren. In every step Rebecca took to ascend to the highest ranks in state government, adviser to a U.S. president, and the CEO of her multi-million-dollar company, she never wavered in the love, nurturing, and caring she provided to her family. She is truly a high-capacity woman in every sense of the phrase.

There's a passage in Proverbs that describes her so well. It says, "A wife of noble character who can find? She is worth more than rubies. Her husband has full confidence in her and lacks nothing of value. She brings him good, and not harm, all the days of her life. … Her children arise and call her blessed; her husband also, and he praises her" (Proverbs 31:10-12, 28 NIV).

This is my Rebecca, and as you read her transformative story, I hope you find encouragement in your own journey and life that truly anything is possible.

David Contreras

Founder, LaunchPad The Center

Beloved husband of thirty-one-plus years

INTRODUCTION

"Start by doing what's necessary; then do what's possible; and suddenly you are doing the impossible."

—ST. FRANCIS OF ASSISI

Pauper to princess...pit to palace...fairytales we tell our children at bedtime to lull them to sleep and help them escape into a world where they can dream big.

But for me as a child, there were no fairytales, only nightmares of a lost girl who desperately searched for her way in the dark, only to find monsters of every shape and kind.

This isn't a book of fiction. It's my story. Growing up I didn't know how to dream, let alone make those dreams a reality. All I knew was survival and a deep desire to break the cycle of poverty, pain, addiction, bad behavior, and poor choices. All I needed was a stable job to get my baby daughter and me off welfare.

A GLIMPSE INSIDE THE JOURNEY

Lost Girl: From the Hood to the White House to Millionaire Entrepreneur exposes the raw truth about my life—the good, the bad, and the ugly—and how I really did go from rags to riches, pit to palace, and pauper to princess (at least feeling like one at times).

So join me in my journey from lost girl to powerhouse success. We'll start at the beginning with the intimate and painful experiences of my past, including unthinkable issues such as child abandonment and sexual abuse. But we won't stay there. I'll also tell you about the unconditional love of a grandmother, my hero, who somehow made everything right. You'll hear the story of my mother's transformation from drug addict to champion, and how she stood by my side when the tables turned and I needed her most. I'll divulge my party lifestyle and the violent rape and attempted murder I experienced after a drug dealer and monster nearly ten years my senior manipulated me into a toxic relationship when I was sixteen and how I got away and eventually erased him from my life.

And we're just getting started.

Strap yourself in because the ride gets wilder. I'll share how I broke away from a physically, emotionally, and spiritually abusive home and started working in a government welfare-to-work program with only a GED. That GED took me from the hood to the Office of the Texas Governor, and eventually all the way to the White House. I'll take you behind the scenes, telling you what it's like to work for the most powerful man in Texas, and then later, for the most powerful man on this planet—the president of the United States—as a special advisor. I'll reveal how I founded a company with no prior business experience and how I turned that business into a multi-million-dollar enterprise.

I had no manual to refer to, no script to memorize and repeat, and no step-by-step program to follow. Instead, I'll describe the unexpected, unsolicited, and powerful transformative moments that took me off a familiar path of dysfunction and destruction onto a new path of focus, grit, faith, and success. I'll show you how I teamed up with mentors and others who believed in me and how they helped me break one glass ceiling after the other with each achievement. No one—and I mean no one—makes it flying solo.

Of course, no good fairytale would be complete without a knight in shining armor. He's in this story too, so enjoy the unfolding of one of the most challenging but greatest love stories of a Texas power couple (so we're told).

And then...

GET READY TO DREAM

My life is proof that bad stuff happens, sometimes really bad stuff outside your control, but dreams do come true, sometimes when you least expect them. Regardless of your past, your mistakes, the roadblocks in your way, your present circumstances, and how lost you feel, it's never too late. The future and the path you choose are what matters the most.

So, turn the page and brace yourself for this bumpy and winding journey from hopelessness to belief, from anger and hatred to the purest love and forgiveness. It's a journey you'll want to take, because even before we get to the end, you'll realize that anything, and I mean anything, is possible, and dreams do in fact come true.

Success is always born out of adversity if people are willing to step outside of their comfort zone and "kill it" in life! It's just waiting for you to come out of the dark so you can find your purpose.

Dream big, work hard, and believe. Then hold on tight and get ready to soar!

CHAPTER ONE

BORN IN FAILURE

"... whenever you get hung up and locked into the past, you're robbing yourself of the present and definitely the future."

—QUINCY JONES

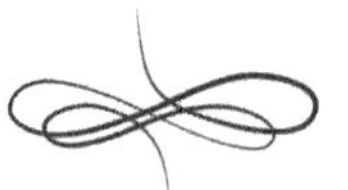

I was born on New Year's Day 1969. For many it is a day full of hope, promises, and resolutions, but for my twin brother, Earl, and me, it was the start of a life full of abuse and trauma, poverty and neglect, rejection and abandonment, unforgiveness and shame. As my mother gave birth to us at a military hospital at Fort Bliss, we had no idea what awaited us on the other side of those walls, but it wouldn't take long before we began learning lessons that no child should learn, seeing things no child should see, and hearing things no child should hear.

Fort Bliss is at the foot of the majestic Franklin Mountain Range in El Paso, Texas. However, my early years were anything but majestic. My mother, Graciela "Grace" Stanley, lived in abject poverty, and by default, so did we. But she did have beauty and plenty of it. At five-foot-eight-inches tall with long, thick black hair, she could stop traffic—cars on the street or those looking for love in a dark bar.

Mom's beauty was matched by her fun-loving, carefree spirit, which did nothing to motivate her to get serious about life, even for the sake of her children. The only reason we were born on a military base was because she happened to be dating a soldier stationed there when she went into labor. Neither she nor anyone else in my family had ever served in the U.S. military.

Instead, Mom was a school dropout. By fourteen, she was already experimenting with alcohol and gateway drugs, then moved on to hardcore drugs like hallucinogens and heroin. These quickly took over her life, and whatever money she earned working odd jobs as a young adult, from dancing to prostitution, she used to buy her drugs.

At nineteen, she had her first child, Daniel. My mother rarely spoke of his father because he had a wife and children., Earl and I were born about eighteen months later. She told us our father was from Yugoslavia, a man named Johnny, with whom she had shared a one-night stand. She met him at one of the clubs where she worked as a go-go dancer. (Back then, you could cross the United States/ Mexican border to party and work, so she often took dancing gigs in Juarez too.)

As I got older, I pushed my mom and grandmother to tell me the truth about my father. Mom finally answered my questions. "Okay," she said. "You wanna know the truth? I'll tell you the truth. You're eighteen now, and I don't want you living your life not knowing."

She gave me the shocking details: My father was the co-owner of the bar where Mom danced. He was also bisexual, and he ran the bar with his gay lover. My mother made a bet with a fellow dancer that she could get Johnny to sleep with her. She won, and Earl and I are the result of her victory. When she found out she was pregnant, she quit her job and never told Johnny about the pregnancy. Because Johnny was married with children, Mom felt strongly he wouldn't want anything to do with the pregnancy.

Although I now had more answers regarding my conception, receiving this new revelation just as I was entering adulthood wreaked havoc upon my self-worth. For the next several years, I believed I was a mistake, and the guilt was sometimes more than I could understand or bear. That's all I know about my father, and neither the original story nor this recent version is inspiring. To this day, my father remains faceless.

When my mother was pregnant with Earl and me, she married a man with the last name of Stanley. My grandmother told me he was a kind and caring man who truly loved my mom. He was willing to raise us with her and take care of her, no questions asked. Three months after the nuptials, however, she had the marriage annulled but kept his last name, which would become my maiden name.

She continued her drug and alcohol abuse, even during her pregnancies. It wasn't as if she didn't know any different; my grandmother begged her to stop using drugs and told her they could harm the babies growing inside her, but Mom didn't listen. Her addictions far outweighed any common sense. She never once feared what this might do to her children. Therefore, Daniel was born under the influence of hard drugs, Earl and I were LSD babies, and my younger sister was an alcohol baby.

Earl and I were also born prematurely and breach, lucky to be alive. My mother had no idea she was having twins until she was in labor. When the doctor told her that her babies were breach and that she was twins, she became hysterical and had to be sedated during our delivery. I'm not sure why she wasn't given a C-section, as she nearly died on the birthing table after delivering us.

My birth weight was only two and a half pounds, and Earl weighed five pounds. He obviously received most of the nutrients in utero. Between my malnourishment and inability to suckle, I spent my first two months of life in the hospital being fed intravenously. My grandmother was the only one who came to visit me as I lay in the clear bassinet, tubes extending from my little body to medical machines. She listened with hurt and frustration as I cried inconsolably for hours from the withdrawal symptoms I was going through.

Later in life, my mother's memories were swept clean of the role her drug use had played in my birth; she remembered only how beautiful I was. Smiling so big with love and pride she'd say, "Becky, when you were born, you had a little perfect button nose. Everything about you was perfect, so tiny, tiny, tiny. I could hold you in the palm of my hand." She'd hold up her palm as a demonstration of my diminutive size. Then she'd say, "I thought you'd break and die because you were so little." Mother was loving in her personality; she just had addiction and mental health challenges that kept her bound.

My grandmother, Keta, confirmed my mother's stories about how tiny I was. She called me a "miracle baby." And my birth was a miracle, but as it turned out, Keta would become a miracle too, an island of safety, love, and stability in the tumultuous waters of my childhood.

THE CYCLE OF DYSFUNCTION BEGINS

Enriqueta Hernandez, lovingly known as Grandma Keta, also never married, which was odd. Her long red hair, green eyes, and five-foot-six build made her a stunning woman. But her skin was her most outstanding physical characteristic. It was flawless and made her look at least a decade younger than she actually was. I am lucky to have Keta's skin genes.

One of eleven siblings, she lived with her sister Hope and Hope's husband, Willie Ramirez, an enormous man who cast an immense shadow, literally and figuratively. At six-foot-six and three hundred and fifty pounds, he was a giant with hands twice the normal size. He had to have his clothes and size-fourteen shoes custom made.

Willie was quite the womanizer in his younger days, a strikingly handsome man of Spanish descent, with thick black hair and mesmerizing blue eyes. However, her brother-in-law was also a violent man, which Keta personally experienced. One time, he held her down at gunpoint and forced her to have sex with him. As a result, she became pregnant with my mother, Grace.

After Grace was born, she and Keta lived in Hope and Willie's home. Hope took care of Grace while Keta worked as a cook at the bus station. The two sisters couldn't have been more different in personality and temperament. Whereas Keta was feisty, bold, and social, Hope was simple, quiet, and obedient. Anything Grandpa Willie said, she did or agreed to. I never heard her even raise her voice to him.

For the first nine years of my mother's life, Willie refused to acknowledge her as his child. Instead, she was told that he was her uncle. Then he found religion and came clean with her when she was nine years old, admitting that she was really his daughter. He then kicked her and Keta out of his house to make things right with his wife, Hope.

Keta never blamed Hope for anything Willie did to her. She considered Hope to be a victim of his abusive and manipulative nature as well. The two sisters stayed very close and never talked about this dirty family secret of how Willie was married to one sister and raped the other, and that a child had been conceived during this assault.

Keta was now forced to live on her own and take care of Willie's daughter by herself. In one respect, it was probably a relief to finally be free from her abuser. In another, she was left with a tremendous amount of dissension, hate, and anger toward my grandfather. And Keta's bitterness toward Willie remained throughout the years. It seeped between the cracks of my grandmother and mother's relationship, creating an environment of dysfunction that spilled over onto and into us as well. In those younger years, we didn't understand the history they shared, the resentment and shame that kept Keta from fully embracing Grace, or the hurt she felt later, watching helplessly as her daughter fell into a downward spiral of addiction and depression. Growing up I just didn't know that there were always many secrets and lies, so many things hidden that had yet to be uncovered.

MOM GOES MAD

Living with Mom involved moving frequently. The government housing program was not tolerant of drug abuse, and my mother was busted several times by social workers for it. We bounced from one project to another in El Paso, and they were rife with crime, including prostitution and drug deals. We moved at least three times before I was six.

Keta lived with us until I was about five. She was the anchor that provided stability despite all the moves. Regardless of where we lived, Mom usually left us while she went to party, and Keta would be there for us. Consequently, she became like a mother to us and acted as a buffer against my mother's negligence and other bad decisions.

In 1972, Mom had taken her bad decisions to a whole new level. Angel dust, a hallucinogenic drug also known as PCP, was the big craze. Mom not only experimented with it but started using it on a regular basis. She was often "out of it," even when she was at home with us kids.

In this particular incident, Mom had consumed too much angel dust, and ended up having a really bad "trip" that lasted for days. Her friends later reported that she had sat in a puddle talking to birds and believed she saw her friend turn into a jaguar in front of her while watching TV. She felt she was in so much danger that she went crazy and had to be admitted to the Big Spring State Hospital, the biggest mental hospital in Texas at the time. I was only three years old.

The doctors found that she had basically lost her mind and had noted "life admittance" on her paperwork, which I still have today. They told Keta that her daughter had fried her brain cells and would never return to mental stability. They declared her completely mentally gone.

So, Mom disappeared from our lives for an entire year. It was a tough time for us all, but Grandma Keta took care of us. Mom underwent shock therapy and lived in a padded cell. She had some violent episodes, constantly tore all her clothes off, and habitually resorted to biting and scratching the attendants while her system detoxified from drugs and alcohol.

Grandpa Willie's sister, Lupe, was the only one able to calm her down, and thus was the only approved visitor. She sang songs to my mother in that padded cell and prayed over her while feeding her and combing her hair. But we were never allowed to visit—not once the entire year. We didn't know where our mother was. Grandma Keta didn't tell us what was going on, other than that our mother was sick. Whether she would return was uncertain.

But Mom surprised everyone. One year later, she miraculously "snapped out of it" and despite her being admitted for life, was released from the mental hospital. She promised Grandma Keta the moon, assuring her that she had quit using drugs and drinking alcohol. But it was just her way of shutting Keta up, getting her off her back and getting her own way.

I was so happy when Mom walked through our front door. She was back home, and we were all together again. Her pale and taut appearance worried me, though. Even at the young age of four, I knew something didn't look right. I'd sit on her lap and hug her tight, hoping it would make her feel better.

Mom did start feeling better. Sadly, she didn't take advantage of her detoxified system. Within a week, she was out on the street again, breaking every promise she had made to Keta.

Of course, Grandma Keta was hurt. She had believed in her only daughter once more, only to again be betrayed with more salt poured into this open wound of broken promises. This hurt turned to anger and unforgiveness in my grandmother's heart for decades to come, right up until just before her death more than forty years later. Her ability to trust had been permanently broken.

RATS, ROACHES, AND ABUSE

Now that Mom was back to her old habits, she constantly left for one reason or another and for no reason at all. I don't recall one night then when my mother was home.

Keta continued her job as a full-time cook at the bus depot, and she couldn't take care of us from early morning into late afternoon. Mom still went out, so she volleyed us around to whoever was available, leaving us at different homes. It's something we had come to expect. The unexpected, however, came when Earl and I fell victim to not-so-nice people that Mom would leave us with.

Two in particular were Mark and Connie, a couple with whom my mother had a close relationship. She trusted them and left us with them on a regular basis. On the surface, Mark and Connie were a nice, church-going couple, which was probably why she felt they were safe. She told us to call Mark "Uncle."

They lived in a tiny hut surrounded by dirt near the border of Juarez. It was full of rats and roaches. We weren't naïve about roaches because we also lived in filth. Mom wasn't clean at all: There were always dirty clothes lying around, dirty beer bottles and food out on the table, dirty dishes piled up. As a result, we had a disgusting number of roaches, so many that I'd have to pick them out of my cereal. Maggots thrived in our trash cans, and flies were the status quo.

Connie was a mean-spirited woman and a strong disciplinarian, often punishing us for minor offenses like messing up the couch or refusing to eat our dinner, things most kids do. She terrorized us by saying, "The rats are going to get you if you don't behave." Sometimes she locked Earl and me in a small dark bathroom for hours with the rats and the roaches—not just any roaches but the large Texas kind, all crawling around. We would curl up, hold each other, and cry.

Connie's threats were emotionally tormenting and exacerbated my fear of roaches and of the dark, scarring me to this day. Even a decade after I got married, I couldn't turn off the light and crawl into bed because I didn't know what awaited me in the dark. I would run and jump into bed, and once there, I tucked my sheet tight under my body because I knew firsthand what might await me. Roaches weren't harmless, not if they were hungry and there were more roaches than food. Oftentimes as a child, I would wake up in the mornings to find large red bumps that itched like crazy. I suspected that roaches had made their way under my covers and bit me.

At some point, Mark began to sexually abuse Earl and me, making us sit on his lap while fondling us, me always underneath my dress. He'd threaten me by saying, "If you tell your mom, I'll hurt you." I was traumatized, as was Earl. Although I was only five years old, I knew that what he was doing was wrong, and I felt dirty afterwards like I had done something wrong. Every time Mom said, "Oh, you're going to stay with Uncle Mark and Aunt Connie," I would cringe, remembering what they had done and fearful it would happen again.

I tried to tell her what Uncle Mark was doing, despite his threats. I would cry, "Mom, they hurt us. They're mean."

It didn't matter. She'd shake her head, purse her lips, and refute my claims. "Shut your mouth," she scolded me. "That's not true. They're nice people. Quit making up stories."

Either she didn't believe Earl and me, didn't want to believe us, or she just blocked it out; I never could tell. It hurt that she didn't believe me, but mostly it left me feeling ashamed. I thought, *Mom doesn't believe me because she doesn't believe her friends can do something so dirty and wrong. But it happened, so it must be my fault.*

Later, as a young adult, I tried to sit down and talk frankly with my mother about my childhood, but the conversation was too painful for her, I think. She denied it again and again. It was easier to reject it and say it never happened than to deal with it.

MY ROCK, KETA, LEAVES

That same year, my mother once again got involved with a violent man, a soldier at Fort Bliss. He beat her when they got drunk together. Alcohol, sex, drugs, and violent men seemed to be mom's way of life. Grandma Keta didn't like the new boyfriend, but Grace was crazy about him despite the black eyes and busted lips. Keta was worried that her daughter would throw caution to the wind and get pregnant with another child she would refuse to take care of.

So, Keta drew a line in the sand in the only way she knew how. She threatened, "Grace, if you end up pregnant again, I'm not going to be around. You're not going to do this to me again. These kids need you." She thought the threat of her absence might force her daughter to finally become a responsible parent, to put her children first. No doubt she was also still feeling the sting of betrayal from Mom's relapse since leaving the hospital a couple of years ago. She probably thought she was enabling Mom's bad behavior by staying around, and actually believed that Grace could get her act together on her own. But, of course, she couldn't. She was struggling with addiction and, as we found out when I became an adult, mental illness that included bipolar disorder.

Mom got pregnant anyway, and Grandma moved out, keeping to her word. I know what a difficult decision it was for her, that she didn't want to leave us alone because we were all so little. (Earl and I were five, and Daniel was almost seven.) She promised us she would be close by, that she would not be gone forever.

Her leaving marked the end of an era for us. We were so close to Grandma Keta. She was the only secure thing we had in our lives, and when she left, the security left with her. To make sure we were taken care of and that someone cooked dinner for us, she took some of her small earnings as a cook at the bus depot and hired a part-time hourly nanny, who came from Juarez, Feli, but it wasn't the same.

Grandma Keta's plans to force mom to change by moving out were made in vain. Mom continued to use drugs. She also brought home men who routinely beat her even though she was pregnant. So we lived with beatings and saw the results—black eyes or fistfuls of hair gone from her head.

Once, at five years old, I awoke to my mother screaming. Thinking she was being hurt, I rushed into the living room and found her having sex with one of her boyfriends in the living room. I had seen this happen frequently, but that did not make it less traumatic to my young and vulnerable mind. Witnessing these things at such a tender age made me very uncomfortable. I instinctively knew that doing this in front of me, in front of any child, wasn't normal.

I covered my ears and tried so hard to pretend I couldn't hear the screaming reverberating through the thin walls of my small bedroom. Not all of them came from Mom, though. Some nights she and her friends would watch horror movies, like *The Exorcist*, on TV and turn up the volume. Each cry of pain and fear filled me with terror. So much violence demonstrated in front of us was more than my young brain could process. I felt stuck in a nightmare of habitual trauma.

Then another social worker busted Mom again for using drugs, and again we were evicted from our apartment. No other apartments were available at the time, or if they were, Mom had already burned bridges with them. We were put on a waiting list for another housing assistance apartment.

With nowhere else to go, Mom's friend Linda offered to let us stay with her until something came through. We packed up the few belongings we had and moved into Linda's double-wide trailer.

Linda was a large and loud woman, but so was my mother. After she quit dancing, she spent her life doing drugs and eating obsessively, so Mom struggled with obesity most of her adult life. Also, Linda had a live-in lover and several children, making the double-wide even more crowded. Altogether, more than ten of us lived in that small trailer at the same time. My mother, siblings, and I shared a single bedroom that was barely large enough to hold a full-size bed. There was no privacy, and we heard and saw many things we should not have.

NEW SISTER, NEW APARTMENT, OLD HABITS

Thankfully, we only had to live with Linda for a few months before another apartment became available, and not a moment too soon. On June 3, 1975, Mom gave birth to my sister, Amber. I was six years old.

Amber was biracial; her father was black, and my mom was Hispanic. She had the most beautiful blue-grey eyes, perfect facial features, and tight locks of curls in her hair with a hint of gold. I would adoringly study her pretty face and think how I couldn't wait for her to grow up so I could dress her up and play house with her.

We had little-to-no supervision after Amber's birth, so Daniel, Earl, and I all pitched in and got used to taking care of ourselves and a new baby. When Mom did stay home in the evenings, many times she'd just bring the party to her. Strangers came and went, living it up to all hours of the night. Often, I woke up in the morning to several bodies sprawled across blankets on the floor, passed out after getting high or drunk all night.

We were now back to having our sleep interrupted by loud music, television, or my mother having sex with abusive men, high as a kite. Full of fear that something bad would happen to me, I did my best to always keep quiet and to myself, to not disturb anything on those evenings. I found ways to escape in my head. My grandmother told me that I was quite the shy, timid young girl. So many times no one even realized I was in the room, but I was an observer. When these scary incidents happened, I sat in a corner, wherever I could find peace and quiet, and held and rocked myself to calmness. Mom would later tell me, "Becky, your favorite position was rocking in the fetal position."

But did she ever stop to wonder why?

MOM ABANDONS US

I remember distinctly the day my mother left. Daniel was seven, Earl and I were six, and Amber was about six months old. That night, Mom had been arguing with Amber's father. And again, he began to beat her. Mom wasn't one to take a beating lying down, so fist fights ensued regularly. Although we hated the fights, they had become the norm with this man.

In this particular fight, Mom and Amber's father started arguing in the bedroom. He stormed down the hallway, and she pursued him as the yelling intensified. We huddled together in our bedroom, trying to ignore what was happening in our tiny apartment. But then a crashing sound—like something had been thrown against the wall and broken—interrupted the screaming. Amber started screaming from her small crib in the corner of our room. I picked her up to console her.

Then the sound of fists hitting body parts penetrated our thin walls.

Daniel, Earl, and I also started crying. "Please stop! Please stop!" we screamed from our room, but to no avail.

"I'm leaving," he yelled, "and I'm never coming back."

Mom's attitude immediately switched from enraged to humble as she begged him, "Please stay." She began telling him how much she loved him.

Then the door slammed.

We ran out of our bedroom and saw Mom reopening the door and yelling, "No, don't leave." Before the door shut behind her, we heard screams and wails and pleas for him to stay as she chased after him.

Finally, there was quiet. Amber stopped crying, and so did we. But that was life as we knew it: yelling, screaming, hollering, crying, and then calmness.

When Mom returned alone, she was quiet, calm, and collected. Apparently, she had pulled herself together. Then she packed her purse and announced over her shoulder, "I'm going to the grocery store."

She walked out of our front door and never came back, abandoning all four of her children. That was the last time we saw my mother for almost two years.

At the time, we thought she'd come back. After all, she told us specifically that she was going to the grocery store. She would often leave for hours at a time, and we had learned to fend for ourselves until she got back. We had essentially become little adults. But that evening, at six years old, I changed my baby sister's diaper and put her to bed alone. I put myself to bed. The next morning, we were still alone. As the morning slowly crept into afternoon that slowly crept into evening, only to repeat the next day and then the next, we faithfully waited for her to come back, anxiously watching the door and staring out the windows, looking for any sign of her.

Finally, after three days in that apartment by ourselves, we realized she wasn't coming back. Daniel knocked on the door of the next apartment. Our neighbor opened it to a little boy staring up at her with fear in his big brown eyes. "My mommy's not home, and we need help," he stated sadly. The neighbor asked him if there was someone she could call, and Daniel gave her Keta's name and number. Keta rushed right over to pick us up. As soon as I laid eyes on my grandmother walking into our apartment, I could finally breathe. I was so relieved and happy to see her, knowing we were finally safe.

It's still difficult for me to talk about today. My mother left her babies alone in that apartment, all helpless and dependent children. I tried to create some justification for her. Was she high? Was she mentally ill? I'll never know.

From the time I was six until early in my twenties, I blamed myself. Perhaps if I had been a better daughter, more obedient, if I'd helped more around the house, she wouldn't have left. What had I done to cause my mother to not want me, to run off? As a child, and as a girl in particular, I needed a mom. When she abandoned us, I lost my self-worth, my self-love. It sent me into a spiral of insecurity and inferiority that lasted into my adult life as I continually questioned, *What have I done?* I struggled with these thoughts until I became an adult and on into my young marriage.

It took some time to come to the point where I no longer believed she intended on leaving for good, that she had just needed to get some fresh air, since she only took her purse with her. Then while she was out, something in her was triggered and told her, "Don't go back," and she didn't. Although I desperately needed to hear this explanation from her, I could never get her to talk about it later in life when I tried so hard to understand why.

Mom wasn't a monster, and I have some gentle memories of her, but it's difficult to reconcile those two people—the mother who combed my hair as I sat on her lap, the mother who told me she loved me all the time, and the mother who allowed us to live in filth, the mother who chose her drugs, alcohol, and men over us. The mother who left her children alone.

When I became a mother myself, I started to realize deep in my heart that my mother did love me and was doing the best she could with the limitations and addictions she had. As an adult, I began to give her lots of grace and forgiveness for those early years. Still, I needed answers for closure. When I asked her questions about our lives growing up, she always answered by saying, "I am both Mom and Dad to you guys. I did the best I could with what I had."

Her response was difficult to accept early on. But as I have aged and matured, I've gleaned a better understanding of her mental health issues and come to grips with her plight.

Perhaps those ten-plus years of hard-core drug use and the electric shock treatments she received in the mental hospital caused irreversible damage to her brain, wiping out some of her memories. It would explain a lot but not everything.

LIFE WITH KETA

Grandma Keta brought us to her small efficiency apartment. Since we had no idea where my mother was or whether she was ever coming back, Keta knew she needed to do something because her place was barely big enough for her. Where was she going to put three children and a baby? So she called the two people she could turn to for help—Grace's father, Willie, and her sister Hope.

"Grace has run off," she proclaimed. "She's left the kids. I have them now."

Hope and Willie had moved to Austin but kept their small two-bedroom house in El Paso, and it was vacant. Grandma Hope told Willie that he needed to let Keta live in it with us kids, but Willie was reticent to give it up. He preferred to keep it empty for "his use" when he visited El Paso, but Grandma Hope put her foot down. "This is how it's going to be, Willie," she decreed. "Keta needs a house for those kids." Grandma Hope finally stood up to Grandpa Willie, which was a big deal, and made it happen for us.

And thus began the best and most normal years of my childhood, living with Grandma Keta in this small house in a regular neighborhood in El Paso for nearly four wonderful years. Grandma and Daniel took one bedroom, and Earl, Amber, and I took the other. We had a real kitchen and a bathroom and a living room. There were kids playing outside. We even established little family traditions that only come with a sense of normalcy and routine. For example, every Sunday, Grandma Keta made a pot roast and cookies or a cake. She was the best cook around! I remember watching her in the kitchen and feeling in awe of her. I wanted to be just like Grandma Keta.

She was poor, but she supported us and gave us much needed orderliness and stability. She paid all the utilities for the house and bought our food, clothes, and school supplies. Keta was also a saver, loving to put aside whatever little left-over money she had. She took a second job every fall, saving every penny to make sure the holidays were special for us. Fortunately, she didn't have a mortgage payment or need to pay rent, thanks to Grandma Hope.

I never once heard Grandma Keta bad-mouth my mom growing up, although as an adult I learned that she had protected me from her negative feelings toward my mother—anger, shame, resentment, confusion, unforgiveness—all the same things that my mother struggled with, and I struggled with later as well. The challenges passed down from one generation to the next were obvious.

Still, I never saw Grandma Keta cry. I never saw her raise her voice. I never saw her angry. She never blamed anyone for anything. She was the most emotionally stable human being I have ever known—an ox, unmovable. Her priorities were love, compassion, and stability. Keta was my hero, and she made a tremendous impact upon our lives. To this very day, when my siblings and I talk about her memory, we call her "Mom Keta."

Although we flourished and thrived with Grandma Keta, I still had a gaping hole left by my mother. So, I made my own new Christmas tradition. Every time someone asked me what I wanted for Christmas each year, I'd respond, "I just want Jesus to bring my mother back home to me."

What made it worse was that no one knew where she was. I would overhear Keta on the phone with Hope, telling her, "No, we haven't heard from her," or "We have no idea where she is. Who knows if she's living on the streets?"

Fear filled my young heart when I heard she might have been alone on the streets. I was concerned she would get hurt and no one would find her, so I prayed that God would bring her back to me, that wherever she was in the world, she was safe.

And I wasn't the only one. Grandma Hope, a woman of great faith, told me she believed God that we would find my mom, that she would be safe and come home. She had been the one who taught me to pray, and now her lesson for me was to take those prayers and apply faith to them.

So many people were praying for my mother—Grandma Keta and Hope and even Willie's daughter, Ida, who was my mother's half-sister—all of us were waiting and hoping and praying during those years for Mom to come home.

MOM RETURNS

Grandma Hope was the one who found her. She and Grandpa Willie just so happened to be in El Paso for a tent revival. They had traveled from their home in Austin, where Grandpa now pastored a Pentecostal church at the corner of Garden and Holly Streets in an inner-city East Austin neighborhood. Before they arrived, however, they got into a car accident. Grandpa Willie got pretty banged up to the point of being bedridden, so he and Grandma Hope stayed with us while he recovered.

Hope decided to go shopping and stopped at the Woolworth's counter for a cup of coffee. As she sat on the stool, she stared at the large mirror behind the counter. She scanned the reflection of other diners in the mirror, then froze as her eyes landed on a young woman drinking coffee a few feet away. The shape of the eyes, the shape of the nose, the profile that was revealed as the woman turned her head when a server dropped a tray—it was all too familiar.

Hope studied the young woman a bit longer. Her heart raced as she realized whom she was watching. *That has to be my Grace*, she thought. *That has to be my Grace*. She really saw Grace as hers, as a second daughter.

But it didn't add up. When Grace had left two years ago, she weighed around three hundred pounds; this woman was tiny, emaciated, about 110 pounds, straight black hair down to her thighs, dressed in a skimpy outfit of fringed tight leather pants and matching jacket.

Despite the extreme disparity in weight, Grandma Hope knew. She walked over to my mother, and they had a wonderful reunion. Years later, Mom told us that was the best day of her life. She admitted to being in bad shape at the time—strung out, hungover, sitting on that Woolworth's stool and contemplating her life and failures. She had literally been living on the streets, and she was asking God for a miracle. Then Grandma Hope showed up.

When Hope came home that afternoon, we were playing outside with some of the neighborhood kids. Daniel was now nine, and Earl and I were nearly eight. A few minutes later, Keta called us inside, and she didn't look happy. Concerned that something bad might have happened, I glanced over and saw Grandma Hope with a huge grin on her face. Confused, my eyes went back to Keta to figure out what was going on.

Keta said, "Grandma Hope has found your mother. She's here in El Paso, and she's fine."

We were ecstatic, jumping up and down and squealing with delight. "When can we see her?" we kept asking, almost in unison.

Amber was now two and a half years old. She watched her older siblings, observing our joy but not joining in. She didn't know who this "Mom" was and didn't understand the excitement. Grandma Keta was the only mother she knew.

Grandma Keta shared Amber's lack of enthusiasm but for different reasons. She gave us a few moments to celebrate before dropping the bad news. Thinking this was another one of my mom's temporary façades, she was upset. She didn't want us to see Mom and didn't want Mom to see us. "Grace needs to clean up her act before she comes back into her kids' lives," she asserted to us all. "I'm not gonna have it. I don't want her around."

She had suffered more than Hope and Willie had from my mother's inability to get clean. Plus, she was protective of us, worried about what it might do to us to be reunited with our mother only to have her abandon us again or to go back into the same cycle of poverty, neglect, and drug abuse.

How quickly we had forgotten it all.

"But Grandma Keta," we started with our defense, "Mom is back! Please, can we see her? Please!"

After realizing how much we wanted to see our mom, she finally relented. "Okay, okay," she said, "I guess the kids can see her, but only if we're there." She pointed to Hope and herself, her raised eyebrows and set jaw telling us that this decision was final.

It was a good thing that Keta agreed since Hope had already arranged for our mother to come see us the next day and told her our address and the closest bus stop. Back then, we didn't have cell phones, and she couldn't call Mom and tell her not to come. She just figured she'd be able to talk her sister into the visit.

I'll never forget the day she returned. It was the happiest day of my young life. I loved my mother so much. I woke up early, combed my hair, placed a big bow in it, and put on my best dress and shoes. I was going to see my mommy, and I wanted to look beautiful. God had answered my prayer, and I was going to have her back.

We all sat in the living room waiting. The bus stop was two blocks from our house, but we could hear the buses pull up and the pneumatic hiss of opening doors. All day I trained my ears to that sound, and when I heard it, I'd run to the front door, swing it open, and look out.

Grandma Hope had said Mom lost a lot of weight, so I knew I wasn't looking for the same woman from two years ago. Time and time again, I'd go and look outside for a thin woman who could be my mom, only to learn that it wasn't her, then again it wasn't her, and again it wasn't her—until it was.

I recognized her right away. She had the same face I used to study when she held me in the past. I yelled, "It's Mom! It's Mom!" I thought my heart would burst out of my chest.

Daniel, Earl, and I darted out the door and ran to meet her. We circled her and hugged her legs. She smelled of smoke and alcohol and other things I didn't recognize, but we didn't care. We had waited for her for so long.

Then fear overcame my joy. I wondered, *What if she rejects me again? What if she pulls away and refuses to accept me?* My feelings of unworthiness did not go away simply because she came back. I had forgiven her, but had she forgiven me for whatever I had done that caused her to leave us in the first place?

Then a hand lightly touched my back...and stayed. My mother was welcoming me, accepting me, and I'll never forget that moment. Mom was finally home, and she wanted me too. All was well with my world. We were her children, and she was our mother. I forgot about all the abuse and pain, the tremendous trauma, the poverty, the screaming and fighting. It all melted away in that moment.

I wouldn't learn until I was a teenager how joyous that time was for my mother. During one of our talks, she admitted, "I was so ashamed as I walked to the house because I didn't know how you kids were going to receive me. I didn't know what you would say, whether you would yell or kick or scream. And you came, you circled me, you grabbed me. All you showed me was love—it was the most demonstrative display of God's love that I had ever seen."

As we walked her to the house, I noticed how sick she was. Her smile couldn't hide her sunken eyes, and her sleeveless top revealed small round bruises connected by a thin line. I didn't know it at that time, but those were track marks created by needles used to shoot up drugs.

As soon as we walked inside, she glanced around and asked, "Where's my dad?"

We pointed to the bedroom down the hall. She rushed to his room with us following behind her like baby ducklings. We witnessed her falling at Grandpa's feet and begging him for forgiveness, and we saw him praying for her.

I had no memories of my mother sober, not for a single day. She had spent the last ten years of her life abusing drugs daily. But on that day, she was delivered from her addiction, and she never used drugs or alcohol again.

Call it a miracle. Call it rock bottom. Call it deliverance. Whatever it's called, my mom had finally had enough.

GONE AGAIN

My mother had come to a place of brokenness, of complete and total surrender as she called out to God. At eight years old, I believed this meant I would have my mother back, that everything was going to be great after that. But that was not how it was going to be.

Within a week of Mom's return, Grandpa Willie recovered nicely and was ready to get back to tent revival or as he called it "saving souls." We were sitting around the dinner table when he announced, "Grace is going on the road with me to preach the gospel and talk about God's miracle in her life. We'll be leaving in two days." He now had an ace card with verifiable proof of God's redeeming power. He wanted to shout it from the rooftops that his prodigal daughter had returned.

As an adult, I can look back and recognize that he wanted to take her on the road, to parade her around the churches and tent revivals, and have her testify to how God had delivered her. I can understand that he probably also wanted her close to him to keep an eye on her. I'm sure that he didn't want to risk her slipping back into her old lifestyle.

But as a child, this was all a slap in the face. Mom was leaving us yet again, and I didn't understand why she needed to go. Furthermore, no one mentioned anything about us going with her. What was more confusing and disturbing was that she didn't seem to put up a fight to stay with us and keep us, except for a weak argument or two. Then she told us, "I'm moving to Austin with Grandma Hope and Grandpa Willie to help him pastor and grow his church and to serve God. That's where God's calling me, and y'all are gonna stay here with your grandmother."

Then she was gone.

It was hurtful, and I felt betrayed and abandoned all over again. But this time, the abandonment happened because "God was going to use her."

Afterward, Mom would visit us about once every other month, making the 1,200-mile round trip to El Paso. She always brought gifts and goodies, but since Mom and Keta didn't get along, she could only tolerate about three days with us. Then she'd be off again.

At the time, I wasn't privy to the behind-closed-door arguments where my mother had begged Keta over and over, saying, "They're my kids, and you need to let me have them," and Grandma Keta's refusal each time: "I'm not gonna let you have them until you prove you're clean. You've only been clean for a few months, and this God situation, I don't care about."

The adults also didn't share with me that Keta had threatened to challenge my mother's custody in court and that my mother had resolved not to fight a legal battle with her own mother. Keta's history with my mom was longer than ours, and she carried more knowledge of past events than we did. She held too many previous hurts and betrayals, and she remembered Mom's many broken promises to change. In her mind, it was still all a big show. She was not ready to send us back.

We stayed with Grandma Keta for nearly two more years. During that time my resentment festered, my anger at God grew, and my questions as to why we couldn't have gone with her went unanswered. But she was still our mom. And this time we knew where she was, and we longed to be with her.

At one point, Mom offered to take Earl, Amber, and me, and leave Daniel with Keta. But Keta said, "If you're gonna rip my heart out, just do it all at once. I'm not splitting them up." After taking care of us for four years, Keta felt like our mother, and we were her children.

But Keta knew enough time had gone by for my mother to demonstrate that she was off drugs, alcohol, and bad men. She saw how much we needed our mother. We were older and not as dependent. She finally relented and allowed us to live with our mom in Austin, in the home she shared with Grandpa Willie and Grandma Hope.

ENTERTAINMENT AND EXORCISMS

I was ten years old and headed into the fifth grade. For me, living in Austin with Mom was going to be an exciting journey and a great life. I was going to be engaged with her, and we were going to be a great big happy family. But it didn't turn out that way.

Instead, I went to live with a woman who was both my mother and a complete stranger. In the two years since Grandma Hope had found her at the Woolworth's counter, Grace had undergone the transformation from drug-addled prostitute to Pentecostal minister and teacher of the Word at *Milagros de Fe*, the Miracles of Faith Church in East Austin. The pendulum had swung from one extreme to the other, and my mother was now enslaved not to drugs but to the church, as well as Grandpa Willie's rules and regulations.

While she was physically more present in our lives now—she wasn't off partying or shooting up—she was emotionally unavailable. She poured her entire self into ministry. We were in church five days a week, and she was in the pulpit half the time. She also traveled with Grandpa Willie for weeks on end, evangelizing at tent revivals all over the Texas valley and into Latin America, giving her powerful testimony to thousands.

It's a story that needed to be told, but it was our story too, and we were still suffering from it. At ten years old, all I knew was that my mother was leaving over and over again for something more important than me.

My anticipation of excitement and a close-knit family turned into a difficult time of adjustments and disappointments. I missed Grandma Keta. She had always supported me and encouraged me, managing to make things better. Now I was on my own, with little adult guidance and support as I tried to figure it all out.

I missed my home in El Paso. For the past four years, I had known where everything was, what to expect and when to expect it. Now I was in a strange city, completely lost. To make matters worse, I was struggling academically in a strange school.

Some of these adjustments were normal for any kid moving to a different city. But all the rules, regulations, and people parading through and using our house for disturbing religious rituals were beyond the norm. At ten years old, I didn't understand why we couldn't live like other families.

When the church service had ended, we didn't just leave church and come home like most. Our home was located conveniently behind the small church, and its congregation consisted of people with significant physical and emotional needs. Every Sunday, they prayed for the sick and the down-and-out.

When prayer didn't seem to work at the church, Grandpa or Mom brought these people into our house after the service ended late at night, most of the time on school nights. They would then continue praying for them for hours on end in our home. These were not physically sick people; they were the ones with mental illnesses or other sicknesses that left them screaming while being prayed over, reminding me of *The Exorcist*. The screams and loud voices from "casting out demons" would wake me up at 11:00 p.m., 12:00 a.m., and sometimes later. At first, I ran into the living room to see what was happening, only to become terrified at the prayer sessions no child should witness. I would go over to Mom and cry, begging her to make it stop. She would brush me off and simply say, "Get back to bed, Becky."

Mom's visitors weren't all sick. She was a social butterfly and loved to cook and entertain church people. That was what Wednesday nights were for. Those mid-week church services ended around 10:00 p.m., and she and Grandpa would invite people over to eat at our house. When this happened, I was made to wash all the dishes by myself, no matter how many there were or what time it was. It didn't matter that I was still a child at ten, eleven, and twelve years old and needed to sleep for school the next day. Mom believed firmly that she was teaching me domestic skills. It wasn't uncommon for me to finish washing the dishes around 11:00 p.m. or midnight. Only then could I go to bed. And Mom had a rule—if you don't do it right the first time, you get to do it all over again. If she found one dirty dish, she took every dish out of the cabinet and made me wash all the dishes in the cabinets. It was her way of teaching me a lesson.

Mom had taken us from late-night drug parties to late-night exorcisms and church dinners, all the while keeping us dirt poor and still on welfare. Though my mother worked constantly in the inner-city church where she ministered, it had no money to pay her a salary. Like always, Mom had yet to hold a regular job and continued to rely on the government welfare system to support us.

Apparently, the church had enough money to pay Grandpa Willie because he was getting money from somewhere. His side of the house we shared was nicely renovated with central heat and air conditioning, nice furniture, and new carpet. But we were never allowed to step inside their living quarters, and Grandpa found a way to make sure he kept us out. He installed a security door between their side of the house and ours and kept it locked.

Although we shared the same house, our living conditions were downright dismal. In the winter, our only source of heat was to light the gas stove, turn it to high, and open the oven door. In the summer, it could be a hundred degrees in the house. We'd have to take cold showers or lie in front of a portable fan on a towel soaked in cold water. Our utilities were routinely cut off. To this day, I don't understand why or how our grandpa could have allowed us to live the way we did in his own home on the other side of a locked door.

Mom wasn't fazed by the filth we had to endure. Our house was infested with roaches—lots and lots of roaches. We learned to wait for them to scurry away when we flipped on the light at night, to step over and around them as we walked down the hall, to shower with our eyes open, and again, to pick them out of our breakfast cereal. Our house stunk from the dog and cat urine that had soaked into the carpet and stained furniture legs yellow. Mounds of animal feces were left on the floor. Fleas leapt up from the sofa, carpet, and the backs of dogs and cats.

We wouldn't have known any better had we not spent four years in basic cleanliness with Grandma Keta, and if we hadn't peeked in and seen the new carpet and furniture each time Grandpa Willie opened his security door to come into our shared kitchen. He and Grandma Hope weren't bothered in the least by our living conditions. They were just there to eat and then return to their abode.

When I told all of this to Grandma Keta—the late nights, our lack, the filth, and how Mom would leave us for weeks at a time—she was appalled. I can only imagine how infuriated she must have been to learn that my mother had taken us out of a comfortable and good life and put us back into a situation that wasn't healthy. She would also ask my mom when they chatted by phone "Grace, why did you take the kids if you're not gonna be home with them?" I would hear them arguing frequently on the phone.

Although we didn't have school supplies in the fall, new clothes, presents at Christmas, or birthday parties, to my mother's credit, we never went hungry. She made sure we had the basics: rice, beans, potatoes, and bread. There was always milk and cheese from the government. She could take these items and create amazing meals from them. I think it was one of the few activities she enjoyed doing, something to distract her from the deep depression that plagued her for her entire life. She would cook for us and feed us. But later, in the evenings, I would hear her crying in her room.

I got glimpses of this side of my mother, the mother burdened with tremendous guilt and shame over the trauma she sustained and dealt with over the years. She never processed it with a therapist or with those closest to her, even with me when I had become an adult. Instead, she packed it away, fearful to acknowledge its existence. But it emerged anyway, showing itself through her neglect during those times when it seemed as if we weren't even there. It came out in the belt beatings she dealt us, in the buckle that landed on our backs or legs when she lost her temper. And it came out during those nights when she cried softly behind the closed door of her bedroom.

Deep down, I suspect that the present added more shame and guilt to her past, knowing that the way she made us live wasn't right, especially with Grandpa Willie living in the same house in much better conditions. She hid all this shame behind a veneer of self-confidence, which was the mother I knew—the one who stood in the pulpit and preached the gospel, who shared her testimony at tent revivals, who whipped up delicious meals even when we didn't have money for groceries, and who smothered us in hugs and kisses and told us she loved us. She hid her shame so well that finally, she hid it even from herself.

When I was in my late thirties, Mom started to show significant signs of mental illness and bipolar disorder. She went into a deep depression for about eight years, all the way up until her death of cancer at sixty-two. I always tell people that cancer didn't kill my mother, her depression did as she lost the will to fight the cancer. Despite my efforts to help her, she never dealt with the trauma in her own life, much less the trauma she created in our lives.

At nineteen, I said to her directly, "Mom, I want to understand why we grew up the way we did, why we sustained so much abuse and neglect."

"Oh no. No, no, no, you didn't—you had a great life," she insisted. "God has been good to us. Don't dredge up stuff that's under the blood of Jesus, that I've been forgiven for. How dare you do that?" She couldn't bear to be reminded. What she never said, what I desperately needed to hear from her was simply, "I'm sorry I hurt you. Forgive me. I was wrong."

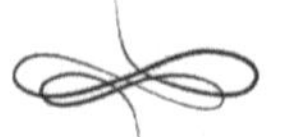

"Your present circumstances don't determine where you can go; they merely determine where you start."

—NIDO QUBEIN

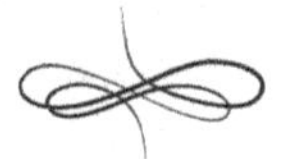

CHAPTER TWO

CHAOS GONE wILD

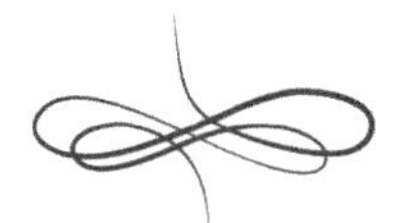

"You had purpose before anyone had an opinion of you."

—**ANONYMOUS**

The grass is not always greener on the other side.

After four years of praying to have my mother back with me, I finally got to experience the "other side," but the grass wasn't even close to being green. That mirage evaporated quickly as life with Mom and Grandpa Willie became more tumultuous and confusing the longer we lived with them.

We had experienced love, nurturing, and guidance from Grandma Keta, but Willie ruled over the house with an iron fist, with Mom fast on his heels. There was no conversation, just rules and religion. No security, just warnings of hellfire and damnation. It was suffocating. I sought solace in my room by listening to music until one day Grandpa Willie barged in and broke all my records and my record player. Within moments he returned with a screwdriver and removed my doorknob, claiming, "I need to keep a better eye on you."

And that he did. Often while getting dressed, I would glance over and see Willie's single eyeball peering through the hole, making sure I wasn't sinning or going against his rules. I was becoming a young woman, and I was conscientious of my body. But now, I was stripped of my privacy, so I had to be on my guard. I had nowhere to go, nowhere to hide my nakedness, so I would turn my back to the door and get dressed in stages, trying my best to cover myself as I went.

Not only was getting dressed challenging (and at times scrutinized), so was wearing the "proper" attire. As a preteen girl, of course I wanted to fit in at school and wear what was cool. Boys started to become more important, and my appearance started to matter.

But Grandpa and Mom weren't interested in fashion as far as I was concerned. Grandpa had certain notions of how a female should and should not present herself (he called "holiness"), and Mom supported them in how she dressed and enforced his rules regarding me. Cutting my hair was not allowed. Jeans, makeup, lipstick, or even a light lip gloss were considered promiscuous. And God forbid I paint my nails. All of it was prohibited, and when I was caught doing any of it, I was punished.

We were forced to practice an extreme religion of the law with a toxic, bondage-driven gospel weighted with rules, rules, and more rules. We were not allowed to live a normal life, and as children, we just couldn't understand why. What our friends in the neighborhood and their families openly participated in—Christmas, Easter, school dances, birthdays, parties, wearing swimsuits to swim, watching TV, listening to the radio, and going to movies—all were from the devil. Those who participated were going to hell.

I wasn't sure I hadn't already arrived.

CINDERELLA

Wanting to engage in normal activities, I flouted Grandpa and Mom's dogmatic rules and did everything I could to make sure they didn't find out.

When I was in the seventh grade, I learned that if I left my house early in the morning for school, I could stop by a friend's house on the way and change out of my long skirt and long-sleeve top into a T-shirt and tight Jordache jeans my friend would loan me. I'd top it off by putting on some of her makeup. Then we'd walk the few blocks to Martin Middle School.

Blending in with my schoolmates built my confidence as more of them seemed to accept me. I felt beautiful for a mere few hours, and some of the guys paid a little more attention to me. Then, like Cinderella, I'd have to scurry off right after school, before my friends could see that my metamorphosis was temporary, and I was a fraud. I'd stop by my friend's house on the way home to change back into my long skirt and long-sleeve top and remove my makeup. Then I'd make the rest of the trip home, and no one was the wiser.

Until they were.

Unfortunately, I had been in a rush taking off my eyeliner at my friend's house and didn't realize it. But Mom did. Her eyebrows furrowed as she studied my eyes. Feeling uncomfortable, I walked away, but not before Mom could interrogate me and announce my crime and sentencing.

"What's that around your eyes?" she yelled after me.

I tried to shrug it off and kept walking. "Nothing." In the solace of my room, I closed the door and breathed a little easier, but only for a moment. Since I didn't have a doorknob, Mom easily barged in, caught me by the arm, and spun me around. She grabbed my chin and pulled my face upward so she could see my eyes. "You're wearing makeup, aren't you? You know that's against the rules. Take off your pants—and your panties. Hold on to the bed," she ordered me.

Denying it only put off the inevitable. I did what she said and then braced myself for the lashes. Mom didn't go easy on me just because I was a girl. She pulled back her arm, and that belt came down hard. Whoosh-smack, whoosh-smack, whoosh-smack. Then I felt the searing pain of metal hitting my lower back.

"You hit me with the buckle!" I cried out in pain.

"Well, who told you to move?" she argued with no remorse in her voice. "If you hadn't moved, then the buckle wouldn't have hit you." Then she gave me a few more whacks.

That was the first and last time I got *caught* wearing makeup. However, it didn't stop me from wearing it. I just learned to wash off every trace of disobedience before going home.

LOSING MY VIRGINITY

I swore to myself that Mom would never hit me again, and I told her as much. This didn't mean I became an angel, the perfect daughter—just the contrary. Although I had been slowly mastering the skills of sneaking out of the house and lying, I wasn't always successful in using them. When getting caught was inevitable, I would run away for a few hours until Mom cooled off.

At least she allowed me to sleep over at friends' houses sometimes. And when she and Grandpa Willie travelled to preach for weeks on end, Grandma Hope would let me spend the night at my friends' houses.

I had spent the night several times with one friend, Priscilla, and gotten to know her parents quite well. She was a few years older than me and "cool." Her parents were also cool, understanding, and of the opinion that "anything goes in their house." They allowed their kids to drink, smoke, and do drugs. They made themselves scarce when their children had friends over so we could openly do whatever we wanted.

One Friday night, Priscilla invited me to stay over. She was expecting several people to come by, including her older brother, seven or eight cousins, and Earl. To me, that sounded like a party! I had never been to a party, so right after school I went to her house and got all decked out in my borrowed party clothes—a tank top and shorts—curled my full hair and applied a full face of makeup. Although barely a teenager at thirteen, I had developed some striking features. Mom would tell me, "You look like your dad, who looked like a model." Wearing makeup just accentuated those features, and on this day, I wanted to look my best.

When Priscilla's twenty-five-year-old brother, Rick, showed up, my heart melted as my eyes fell upon his handsome light-skinned face that contrasted with his dark hair. He too wore a tank top, revealing the muscles on his five-foot-eight frame.

We started flirting with each other. I'd catch him looking at me, and then he'd look away. Wow! This older guy was interested in *me*! Each flirtatious glance and smile boosted my confidence level. It didn't take long before everyone started having fun, laughing and joking around with each other. Then Rick walked over to the bar and started mixing drinks. He looked up at me with that beautiful smile. "Hey Becky, have you ever drunk alcohol before?"

I glanced down and shook my head, feeling embarrassed by my admission. Then a glass nudged my hand. "Here," he encouraged. "Try it."

I looked up into his eyes, and he returned my gaze. He handed me a glass, and I took it. The liquid warmed my throat as it travelled down, and I could feel it coating my stomach. Even better, I found that things that had bothered me before didn't matter anymore. My inhibitions started to dissipate, and I actually started to feel happier. I loved the undivided attention Rick gave me, and as the night wore on, he gave me more and more.

After I finished that first drink, he took my glass and refilled it. *Well, if one drink made me feel this good, I can only imagine what another one would do*, I rationalized. I had another glass and then another. It wasn't as fun anymore as the room became fuzzy. Rick took me by my hand and led me to his bedroom. Even drunk, I wondered if this was a good idea.

He observed my reluctance. "Hey, it's no big deal." He shrugged. "All we're going to do is watch TV in here for about an hour. There's a really funny show that's coming on that I want to watch with you." Wow! He wanted to watch a show with *me*! Quite thrilled, I pushed aside what little reservations I still had and agreed to watch TV in his room. He locked the door behind us.

My inhibitions started to resurface when I heard the click. I spun around to ask him what he was doing but instead stumbled, almost falling over. Reading my mind, Rick said, "Relax," in an encouraging voice. "I'm only locking the door so that no one barges in and interrupts this show." He then led me to the side of the bed. "Here, sit down." When I hesitated, he added, "I don't bite."

He sat next to me and softly tucked my hair behind my ear. I had never been in a situation like this, and I wasn't in the right frame of mind to process it. He made me feel good, beautiful, and worthy, something I had not felt before…ever. When I gave no resistance, he kissed my ear, then my cheek, and then my lips. After a few moments, he lightly pushed me back on the bed and undressed us both. I again offered no resistance.

Early into the encounter, I started to whimper and cry from the pain. I think it made him nervous, afraid others would hear me and bang on the door to find out what was going on. He got up, got dressed, and left the room, leaving me there on the bed feeling completely lost. After what seemed like hours, even though it was just twenty minutes, I also got up and dressed, wiped the tears from my eyes, pulled myself together, and went back to join the party with my friend.

When I saw Rick back in the group, I briefly froze and searched his face for that beautiful smile. He stared back at me with a smirk on his face instead. I looked away and didn't pay him much attention from then on, and I never breathed a word of it to my friend or her mom. At thirteen, it was simply one of the first steps in a terrible journey for me, down a bad road of dating much-older men and devaluing myself through promiscuity.

When I allowed my virginity to be taken by a man ten years my senior who was almost a stranger, I believed I was no good and that nobody cared for me. But in that moment, Rick had made me feel good about myself, something I never got at home and was starving for. I had never known the love of a father or the healthy love of a male figure in my life. I desperately needed to feel loved. Having the attention of a man felt good, even if for a short time. I needed to be valued by somebody, by anybody, and Rick was there to take advantage of me and fill that void. The only person I felt had ever loved me and truly cared about me was Grandma Keta, and she wasn't around anymore. Consequently, I built a wall of resistance to anything healthy or normal.

SHAMED AND CONDEMNED

Our lives were wrapped around Grandpa Willie's church, or perhaps the church was wrapped around our lives, or maybe both. Regardless, it was all-consuming; we were always there whenever the doors were open, sitting in the pews, listening to each sermon. At over 350 pounds, Grandpa Willie couldn't stand for long to preach, so he would sit in a chair on the platform instead. Either those who needed prayer knelt before him or his chair would be carried and placed amid the people where he could grab them and pray for them.

During one of his revivals when I was thirteen, the small church was packed. Grandpa Willie sat in his pulpit chair, ranting about sin and how it led to hell. Feeling convicted for secretly experimenting with pot and alcohol, I came forward to repent, which was normal. In fact, I came forward each Sunday because I had been told the whole preceding week that I was a sinner. The daily services held during the revival only gave me many more opportunities to atone for my sins.

I walked to the front of the church for prayer and repentance, and Grandpa Willie pulled me up onto the small platform. He turned me around so the congregation could see me, and I them. He then interrupted the altar call. "Excuse me, everyone." He glanced around the small sanctuary as everyone became quiet and turned their attention to him.

I stood frozen, not knowing what was going to happen. Was he going to proudly announce that his thirteen-year-old granddaughter had accepted Jesus as her Savior? Not a chance. He had fixated on my little gold ankle bracelet, a gift from a friend at school. "As most of you know, this is my granddaughter Becky. See the bracelet on her ankle?" Everyone's eyes dropped to my ankles. "Our Becky must be a prostitute who doesn't even try to hide her trinket of sin and fornication."

Some gave a small gasp and placed their hands over their mouths in shock. I couldn't tell if they were surprised to hear him make that ridiculous comment or to learn about my "sin." Mom was standing with them near the altar, so I begged her with my eyes to help, to do or say something. Her mouth was slightly ajar, and her eyes were wide open in disbelief while she too stared at my ankle. Then she looked into to my terrified face, and her eyes softened with care and concern. Humiliated and shamed, I wanted to run out of the building right then and there and go hide my filth. But Grandpa had a firm grip on my shoulders. I wasn't going anywhere until he said I could.

Later that night after the service, I overheard my mother recalling the incident on the phone with Aunt Ida, her sister who lived in Midland. She cried as she told her how furious she was at Grandpa Willie for shaming me in front of everyone. Feeling a bond with Mom over a shared injustice, I thought for sure she would take action and set Grandpa Willie straight. Instead, she hung up the phone, walked over to me, hugged me, and said, "Becky, never wear that ankle bracelet in front of your grandfather again."

From then on, I began sneaking behind their backs even more.

Unfortunately, my mother felt powerless to fight Grandpa, to push back, to tell him he was being too strict with us. After becoming a young adult mom myself, I recalled her telling me of the abuse she had also sustained by Grandpa Willie in her youth. Despite it, Mom was so committed to him; it was like she worked double-time to earn his love, affection, and acceptance. But the harder she worked, the more he rejected her. Publicly, however, "Daddy" could do no wrong. She honored and revered him just like all his other congregation members.

Earl, Daniel, and I couldn't fight Grandpa Willie either, so we pushed back, taking power in the only way we knew how—we began stealing from him.

LITTLE DEVILS

During those times when Grandpa Willie, Grandma Hope, and Mom were in church, we'd sneak out the back door that led to our living quarters and the church office on Grandpa's side of the house. After several attempts, we figured out a way to get in and out of the church office without anyone knowing it.

We snuck in every couple of weeks. Each time, we stole things. Little things in the beginning, mostly—treats and dollar bills from the offering plate. We knew that he knew it was us stealing from him and the church. For us, it wasn't as much about the money as it was the satisfaction of getting revenge. But it only enraged him. Whenever he noticed something missing, he stormed into our side of the house like a raging bull. He'd fill the kitchen with his deep, loud voice. That was our cue to run and hide behind our mother, because she did stand up for us sometimes in little ways.

"Little devils!" he'd scream at Mom as he wagged his giant finger in her face. "Your devils! Those kids of yours are stealing from me again! I'm going to catch them, and when I do, I'm going to beat them."

"My kids would never do that," she'd assert. "You're always accusing them of being devils. You are so wrong. They've been over here all day."

On one occasion, he glared over Mom at Daniel with a mixture of anger and hatred. "That one right there." He moved his finger from Mom's face and pointed it at Daniel. "It's him. I'm going to punish him if you don't." His large body leaned toward my brother, making me fearful that he was going to take matters into his own hands right then and there. And he might have if Mom wasn't in the way.

My mother knew he spoke the truth. She could verbalize her protests, but the words never translated to action. Grandpa Willie was too huge, too menacing. After all, he did provide a roof over her head. So despite her occasionally admitting that he was hard on us, she always ended up bending to his will.

"I'll deal with it, Dad. Please leave us alone." Her voice remained calm.

My grandfather's eyes darted between my brothers and me as he contemplated her request. Then he turned and walked through his door and slammed it shut. Once we heard the clicking of the locks, we let out the deep breaths we had been holding in.

My mother turned to my older brother with tears streaming down her face. "Daniel, you know what you have to do."

We all stared at her in horror. Daniel was fourteen years old. Was she really intending to spank him?

Daniel searched her face as he processed her request. Then he walked to her room. He came back with a belt, his shoulders hunched over, and reluctantly handed it to her.

She didn't waste any time letting him have it. With every strike, my body jerked as if I too were being hit. With each whoosh and smack of the belt landing on his body, more tears escaped from my eyes. He squirmed and cried until he gave up and lay there flinching while she continued to beat him. When she was done, she was breathing hard from the exertion. The belt's buckle created welts on his back and legs that bled as all of us, including Mom, cried.

Quietly, she left and returned with a wet cloth and ointment, and she began to tend to his wounds. Daniel stared at her with such intense hatred, and I realized I was doing the same. So was Earl.

In that moment, we lost all respect for her. We had never been able to understand how she could be so loving and so hateful at the same time, but from then on, we stopped trying to figure it out. It was a turning point for us. And that's when the major teen rebellion began.

SUFFERING FROM UNDIAGNOSED ADHD

Another thing I couldn't figure out was school. I couldn't sit still, pay attention, and study. I struggled to comprehend and retain what I was taught, and my testing skills were poor no matter how hard I prepared beforehand. One of my teachers in middle school told me, "You'll never amount to anything because you're stupid." I took that in and believed it. My mother never showed interest in my studies. She rarely asked, "Do you have homework?" If she didn't ask, I didn't care. My grades plummeted. Mom's focus was elsewhere, so she offered no help, and I didn't know how to bring them up on my own.

My learning issues haunted me into my adult years. I needed to find out why. Out of sheer frustration, I conducted my own research and realized I had been suffering from attention deficit hyperactivity disorder (ADHD) all my life. ADHD is treatable, but until I recognized it for what it was, it made everything in my life challenging or in many cases impossible.

While in school, not knowing or understanding my challenges left me to believe the only explanation I had been given up to that point—I would never amount to anything because I was stupid. So I quit fighting against what seemed to be unsurmountable odds. I no longer cared about school. I was tired of beating my head against the wall and not getting anywhere.

As a result, later on in my freshman year, I got involved with a bad crowd. They welcomed me. Even better, it was easy and cool to be an underachiever with them.

Together with my brothers, we broke into local east Austin factories and stole cases of snacks, such as corn chips, and beer.

Of course, we continued stealing from Grandpa Willie when the opportunity presented itself. But when I was fourteen, the worst happened—Grandma Hope died suddenly in her sleep. We were later told that her passing was due to severe diabetes. To add to our grief, only a few months after her death, Grandpa Willie married the twenty-something-year-old church secretary.

The marriage was a slap in Mom's face. She assumed that because it happened so quickly, there must have been an affair going on between the two of them while Grandma Hope was alive, and she thought of Hope as her second mother. Fortunately, Grandpa Willie and his new wife weren't around much, traveling back and forth between Austin and El Paso.

Still, the pain was too much for Mom. She left Grandpa Willie's church and started attending another one called Templo Sinai.

My brothers and I continued down our path of rebellion, though. By the time I turned fifteen, Daniel taught me to drive his sports car. I'd take Earl, still my best friend, to night clubs using fake IDs. Every night we snuck out to one party or another—seven days a week of all-night party chaos. One time, when Daniel was out of town, I even took his car out by myself and wrecked it.

Mom noticed us creeping back into the house in the wee hours of the morning after returning from a night of mischief. In an effort to deter us, she started locking the doors at midnight, so we just rigged a window in my room that allowed us to sneak in whenever we wanted.

One early morning after I'd been drinking and drugging all night, Mom stormed into my room furious. At fifteen years old and with a chip on my shoulder, I no longer cared. As she started yelling at me, I responded, "Mom, I'm tired. I don't want to talk."

She slapped me across the face. The sting of that slap was both physical and emotional. Something in me snapped the moment her hand landed on my face. That was the pivotal instant when my mother lost control of me. I stared at her and realized my eyes no longer projected any emotions but reflected how I really felt inside—dead. "Are we done here?" I asked stonily. "Because I'm done."

And I was. Mom's eyes revealed realization and terror at the same time. I believe she knew she had lost me completely with that slap. She started crying and said, "I feel like I've lost you! I don't know what's wrong with you or how to reach you." She rushed off to her room upset, but I didn't care. I wanted her to feel the pain of rejection that she had made me feel for years.

The following year, I rejected her the best way I knew how—I moved out with Earl. Even thought I was only sixteen, I got a job as a cocktail waitress after lying about my age. I made a lot of money in tips, but then I blew it on drugs, alcohol, parties, and clothes. Three months later, with our tails tucked between our legs, we came crawling back to Mom.

Why did she let us come back? I've often wondered. When we did, she embraced us and welcomed us in, just like Grandma Keta had done for her. Once she realized she'd lost her grip on us, I think she knew that all she could hope for was to pray for us and support us however she could. She started treating us differently. No longer did she insist on enforcing her rules or belting us. She didn't get mad or upset when we stayed out late either. Instead, she would fall on her knees and cry out to God on our behalf. So many times, when I came home late, I'd find her in my room at 3:00 or 4:00 in the morning, kneeling at the foot of my bed and praying for me. As soon as she saw me come in the window, she would help me get into bed and say goodnight.

We were her prodigal children. She was hoping that we would "come home" and experience the kind of miracle she had in her own life.

She tried to reconnect with me and often pleaded with me to open up to her, but it was too late. She had put everyone and everything before my siblings and me—God, church, Grandpa Willie, the congregation. Our foundation was decimated, and we had no solid ground from which to build. So I sought attention elsewhere, and I found it in the most dangerous of places.

THE START OF A TOXIC RELATIONSHIP

At sixteen, I was tall and slim with strawberry-blonde hair and legs that wouldn't quit. Earl and I had been strength training at Gold's Gym and engaging in two- to three-hour dance-offs in the club four days a week. I was in the best physical shape ever, no longer the skinny girl with the immature body. The summer before my junior year, I'd go to the community pool, not so much to swim as to show off my swimsuit (and me in it) and work on a tan.

The lounge chairs filled up fast, and on this particular day the only one left was just inside the gates. As I lay there soaking up the rays, I heard someone on the other side of the fence talking. I turned my head toward the voice to find that the one-sided conversation was directed at me. Sitting up, I shielded my eyes from the sun's glare and saw an older Hispanic man, short, about twenty-four. By his wide smile, gaze of admiration, and lighthearted compliments, I could tell he was flirting with me.

He introduced himself as Juan. I had seen him around; it was hard not to notice the brand-new sports cars he drove and the trendy clothes he wore. Clearly, he had lots of money. So, although he was not the usual type of guy I'd go for, he definitely had my attention.

After several minutes of shallow conversation, Juan asked me out. I accepted. He picked me up that night in his Porsche. He told me that he owned this one and several others in addition to the one I'd seen earlier at the pool. I had never been in such an expensive sports car, so the date already started off special. I soon discovered I loved fast cars because they made me feel free.

Juan took me to an extremely nice and expensive restaurant. He walked, talked, and looked confident. Despite his shorter stature, he owned the room with his personality. He was also a big tipper and ordered the best high-end drinks, so the wait and bar staffed loved him and kept the drinks coming.

After that first date, he handed me a couple of hundred-dollar bills. "Use it for you," he said, "for your mom…whatever." What impressionable sixteen-year-old wouldn't fall for him? Well, this one did immediately. Hook, line, and sinker! The minute I came home, I showed Mom that wad of cash, and she got suspicious. But I was too excited to heed any of her concerns. She just hadn't gotten to know Juan yet. He was so nice.

He paid attention to me, something I was still desperate for. He was taking me out on the town several times a week, driving me around in a different sports car each time, loading me up on drinks, surprising me with dozens of roses in every club we visited, buying me nice clothes and jewelry, and giving me a sizeable weekly cash allowance.

After a while, his true colors started to show, and I started noticing that Juan was a diabolical man—controlling, manipulative, and womanizing. He believed he ran the East Austin community and owned the streets. Everywhere we went, people revered him as a "bad ass," a reputation he relished earning. To me, he started looking more like a thug than the debonair man I had initially become infatuated with. It wasn't enough to make me stop dating him though.

Then, six months into the relationship, I found out that Juan was married with children and dealing drugs. I confronted him, but he denied it. "Don't worry, babe," he assured me, "You're number one for me. I'm going to take care of you, and I'm gonna protect you. You're safe with me. No one's gonna mess with you because I've put the word out on the streets that you're my girl." But I had already caught Juan in numerous lies and discovered he had fooled around with one of my friends. This latest news of his marriage was too much. I tried, albeit weakly, to break it off.

He wouldn't accept the breakup, so he stalked me. He sent me flowers and drove by my house every day. After a few weeks, he bought me a car. Little by little, he wore me down until I finally chose to ignore every instinct I had deep inside to run, and I began my journey to hell with him.

My mother was furious! She couldn't stand Juan. He was a sweet talker with women and could talk his way into and out of any situation. But it didn't work with Mom. He tried to bring her gifts to buy her affection, but that didn't work either. She'd say, "He's a snake. I don't trust him. Something's not right about him."

Mom could dislike him all she wanted, but Juan was my ticket out of poverty and out of East Austin—the hood, as I called it. I planned to enjoy the ride and let him take care of me. After all, a girl could do worse. He was a much older man by almost ten years—the male figure I never had in my life to give me attention and care—and I liked it. Desperate for a different life, I became hardened to how I got it. Deep down, though, I think I knew there'd be a price to pay for all of these things. Until then, I turned a blind eye to all his flaws. By that point in my life, I had devalued myself in such a way that it didn't matter how he treated me. I was used to being treated like crap; it was common. Because I had no pride or love for myself, I just sunk deeper into his control and death-grip.

The longer we were together, I began to learn things about Juan that scared me. He wasn't just any drug dealer; he was one of the biggest drug dealers in the area.

He had a huge network of people who relied on him, as well as other dealers who worked beneath him.

We had been dating for almost a year when he put me up in an apartment, which allowed me to move out of my mom's house. I was seventeen. He wanted to have me all to himself and be able to spend the night together without needing to bring me home late at night. He also wanted his escape from his wife on the side.

While hanging out at my apartment one night and drinking, he took charge of his new level of control. "Becky, I don't like you working at the club because of all the men around you. I want you out of there."

I was taken aback. Thinking he was being silly, I became defensive. "But Juan," I explained, "my job as a cocktail waitress includes being nice to men and serving them drinks. Stop being jealous. You can't control me."

He wasn't hearing it. He didn't like me telling him he couldn't control me. He was drunk and snapped. He screamed, "I want you to quit right now!"

I argued in return, but he wasn't backing off. The longer he stayed that night, the more upset he got. The disagreement turned into an argument, which turned into an all-out fight. I had seen this rageful side of Juan before, but it had been directed at other people. Now, it was directed at me. I understood then why he had come to my job at the club a few times and created trouble. I understood the repeated warning from a bouncer I worked with who was protective of me who would say, "I know Juan. Watch your back. I don't want you to be found dead somewhere if you can't get away from him."

Fear rushed in, and the only thing I knew to do was to break it off again, but this time, it almost cost me my life. He raped me that night and tried to choke me to death. Fortunately, he freaked out when he saw my face turn blue from the lack of oxygen. He later told me that my look of fear and gasping for air freaked him out, so he released me before it was too late.

He justified his violence, of course, and then used it as another tool of control. "I'm only upset because I love you, Becky. You belong to me. If you ever try to get away from me, don't you think for one minute I'll let anybody have you," he threatened. "I'll cut up your pretty little face so badly, no one will ever want you."

I should have listened to the bouncer; I should have listened to Mom. At just seventeen years old, I realized what a dangerous web I'd become entangled in and how powerless I was to leave.

SEVENTEEN AND PREGNANT

Naturally, I was distraught and fearful, so I went to Mom's to tell her what had happened. She no longer shared a house with Grandpa Willie. Around the time I moved to the apartment Juan had rented for me, Willie's new wife kicked Mom out. Fortunately, she had somewhere to go. Willie allowed her to live in one of his small houses about four blocks away, even though it was a dump.

Standing at the sink in her tiny kitchen, I pulled down my turtleneck and showed her the fingerprints Juan had left on my throat. "He tried to kill me," I whispered as I momentarily relived that moment.

She gasped as her eyes filled with tears. "Oh Becky," her voice cracked and then became angry. "How dare he do this to you! I knew there was something wrong with him. He's dangerous! I'm just going to have to pray. I'm going to pray him right out of your life, for him to be caught and sent to prison."

But Juan didn't disappear from my life, and Mom's prayers had lost credibility with me. Instead, that same year, in the winter of 1986, I became pregnant with his child, and I was catapulted to a new level of ownership by him. Juan already two other women with which he had fathered children—his current wife and ex-wife—and now he had a third, a mistress to control.

I didn't want a baby. I was only seventeen and a junior in high school, nowhere ready to be a mom, and I was afraid of the father. I saw that baby as a chain that would lock me into an abusive, toxic, controlling relationship forever.

I decided to get rid of the baby. First, I had to break the news to my mother, and then I asked her for help. She refused, of course, and forbid me to have an abortion. Instead, she pulled out all the stops to try to get me to move in with her and have the baby. She told me, "Life is a precious gift from God, Becky. Please consider your life. Maybe this is a way for you to get it on track. I'll help you. Please let me help you."

Her offer didn't provide a solution to my dilemma. The last thing I wanted was to move in again with Mom, back into that poverty-stricken and dirty environment, and, as I saw it, rule-oriented house of bondage. Even though Earl stayed with Mom now and then, Daniel had joined the U.S. Marine Corps, so he wouldn't be there.

Then Mom told me she let Grandpa know I was pregnant and asked for his help. He had responded, "She can flush that baby down the toilet for all I care. That baby will be born in sin, and I don't want anything to do with her." His words not only caused me to hate him more, but they confirmed that I didn't want to move back and give Grandpa something else to shame me with. Lost, confused, and alone, I tried to terminate the pregnancy in other ways. Some of my "loser" friends gave me suggestions on how to abort a baby, thinking they were helping. One told me that if I drank a fifth of Jack Daniels and then smoked a bunch of pot, I would miscarry. I tried it; it didn't work. I tried everything else I knew, no matter how illogical it sounded. I could *not* have this man's baby. Doing so would be signing my own death warrant or, more tragically, forcing me to suffer through a life of hell on Earth.

I continued living the way I had been, abusing alcohol and drugs all the way through my first trimester. I even got to a whole new level of stupid and threw myself out of a moving car. Through that time, my mother begged me to stop, to take care of myself, to think of my baby. Sound familiar? Mom and I were repeating history—her begging me to stop the way Grandma Keta had begged Mom to stop two decades before. I'd think, *Who is she to tell me what to do?* In my mind, she had no room to talk.

After the third month, I started to show. When I realized that I wasn't going to miscarry no matter how I abused my body, I surrendered to my mother's care and moved back in with her. Then just like Grandma Keta, my mother swooped in and promised to protect and raise her grandchild.

Ashamed and fearful that my friends would see me pregnant, I dropped out of high school before finishing my junior year, and Mom didn't encourage me to stay. I was still struggling in my classes and had lost confidence in myself, so I didn't care. Back then, girls who got pregnant while in school were given few options. Today, high schools have wonderful programs including on-site daycare to help teen moms stay in school.

I was now back in a little room. I reminded myself that it was temporary, just long enough for Mom to help me get through the next six months. And help she did! She was amazing during that time. She took care of me, helped me get off drugs and alcohol for the remainder of my pregnancy, and even kept Grandpa Willie away from me. Six months later, my daughter, Crystaline, was born. Miraculously, although I had abused my body the first trimester, she was a healthy and perfect child.

When I first laid eyes on her in the hospital, I couldn't believe such a beautiful baby could have lived inside me for nine months. I broke down crying at the thought of getting rid of her. I was her mother, and I should have been protecting her, not trying to destroy her. Yet here she was, flawless in spite of me. She was a miracle angel sent by God to help me get on track.

Holding her in my arms in the hospital and looking into her innocent eyes, I promised her the moon. "I'll love you and care for you. I'm going to get my life together. I'm going to change." My well-intentioned promises lasted about two weeks.

LIKE MOTHER, LIKE DAUGHTER

When Juan saw Crystaline, he wanted her immediately. She was as stunning as a porcelain doll. He claimed my lifestyle was no way to raise a child (as if his was) and insisted that I allow his wife and family to raise *my* daughter.

Mom would not have it. She put her foot down and said, "Absolutely not! As the sperm donor, he has no say in the matter." She called him "the sperm donor" because to her, he was no father and didn't deserve that title.

I agreed with her and told Juan, "Mom's going to help me, so it's all good."

Mom also refused to let me list him as the father on the birth certificate. To this day, Crystaline's birth certificate reads "Father unknown." In hindsight, that was the best advice my mother could have given me, and I'm so glad I followed it!

Even though she had helped me, living with my mom felt suffocating and restrictive, and now that the baby was born, I wanted nothing to do with her rules. Two weeks after I gave birth, I left Crystaline with my mother and returned to another apartment Juan rented for me and to my job as a cocktail waitress. (Juan tolerated my job as long as he was present to monitor me throughout my shifts.)

I also reclaimed the keys to the car that Juan had given me. It was all too easy to slip right back into my old party lifestyle.

Most of all, I abandoned myself to a sea of shame, fear, hate, and unforgiveness for myself, and I was drowning in it. I couldn't seem to free myself from the all-too-familiar destructive generational patterns, habits, and behaviors, so I just stopped trying.

Over that next year, my mother raised my daughter. At times she brought Crystaline to my apartment to visit, hoping that if I spent time with her, I'd be more inclined to change for her, to be a mother to her. But I was too caught up in myself to notice how precious Crystaline was. She was transforming from a tiny newborn into a happy baby. Her slate-gray almond-shaped eyes had turned to twinkling brown, and she had inherited her great-grandmother Keta's beautiful porcelain skin.

Mom dearly loved her granddaughter and took a personal interest in caring for her every need. She poured her life into her, and for that I am forever grateful. In those early years of Crystaline's life, Mom redeemed herself to me. In her way, she felt she had a reason to live and thrive. She had finally become a real mom and made sure my daughter lacked nothing. She even mastered the art of shopping at the used-clothing boutiques as she still struggled financially and had to make every dollar count. You would have never known it because Crystaline was always dressed in the most adorable baby outfits. Sadly, I was so stuck in a rut of selfish behavior during Crystaline's first year that I didn't contribute one penny to help Mom raise her.

My daughter felt loved, though, and naturally she reciprocated. She adored her Grandma Grace, or "Mom Grace" to her in that first year. Mom knew better than most that I was throwing away my life, including a relationship with my daughter, and she became relentless in her efforts to get me back on track "for Crystaline's sake." At times, she could be quite annoying, but I think that was her goal.

For instance, Crystaline was about eight months old when Mom decided to pop over to my apartment unannounced with her. Unfortunately, I had come home late after working at the bar and then partying until four that morning. I had been asleep just a few hours when someone started banging on my door. I was quite hungover, and each pound caused my head to hurt more. Irritated, I wondered who could be bothering me. Then I heard a familiar voice through the door. "Becky? It's me, Mom, and Crystaline. We're here to see you."

I tried to ignore her, hoping she'd give up and go away, but she didn't. She banged on that door for maybe fifteen minutes nonstop. Now I was infuriated. Who was she to come by anytime she wanted and expect me to be available? I rushed to the door and hastily threw it open. I glared at Mom, but she was unfazed as she held *my* daughter. My eyes then fell onto Crystaline looking cute as a button in a red polka-dot dress with a red bonnet. I smiled at her, forgetting all about my anger at Mom, but it was too late. When Crystaline saw my scowl, she screamed and clung to my mother, refusing to let me hold her. Mom said, "Becky, one day, you are going to have to grow up and take care of your daughter. She needs you, so please snap out of it!" Crystaline continued to scream and scream until my mother finally relented and took her back home.

Later that evening, I replayed that incident repeatedly in my head. It reminded me of another time when I was fourteen years old and yelling at my mother, telling her that I would never abandon my own children the way she had abandoned us. Never. Now here I was, only four years later at eighteen, a stranger to my own daughter, strung out, lost, in poverty, and ashamed. I had done the one thing I vowed I would never do—abandon my child—because the scars of that rejection, a life of living in humiliation and addictions, had never faded.

To numb the pain that night, I drank more than usual. That was my mode—feel pain, drink, do drugs. Abuse of substances made it all go away…for the time being. I didn't know how to change it, though. I didn't know how to escape. I still couldn't forgive my mother, so how could I forgive myself for doing the same thing?

THE FACE IN THE MIRROR LOOKING BACK

My remorse lingered, but I didn't wallow in it. I went right back to the party life, my apartment full of people until 2:00 or 3:00 a.m., whooping it up and having a good time. During one of my parties, after drinking and doing drugs all night, I stumbled into the bathroom and flipped on the light. There staring back at me in the mirror was my mother's face. I jumped back at the sight.

The image was so real; it wasn't due to the drugs and alcohol. Quite the contrary. It actually sobered me up! My mother stared at me from my bathroom mirror, refusing to go away. It wasn't the plump, happy face of my mom that day but the boney, sunken, sad face on a ninety-pound frame that greeted me at age five when she returned to us after her life on the streets. I flashed back to her story of attempted suicide when she was living on the streets in Juarez and what had led up to it. According to Mom, she was in a friend's bathroom, high on hallucinogens and gawking at herself in the mirror. Instead of her own face looking back at her, she saw a bare skull and knew it was death.

She told me that a voice came out of the skull and spoke to her. "Look at yourself, Grace. You look like death. Your children don't know where you are. Not even a dog would abandon her puppies, yet you've abandoned your kids. You've got to kill yourself." Devastated, she took a razor to her wrists. Her friend found her in a puddle of blood and rushed her to the hospital.

Mom was older than me when her "mirror experience" happened; I was only nineteen when I had mine. It scared the hell out of me. Terrified, I rushed through my apartment and kicked everyone out, including my twin brother who was staying with me that weekend.

It was a wake-up call. Right then and there, the desire to change my life was born. I was still tethered to Juan, however, and I didn't know what to do about it. But shortly after that incident, as suddenly as he'd appeared in my life, Juan was removed from it. I was watching TV when the man who had held me in his grip since I was sixteen appeared on the screen. Two men wearing dark-blue jackets and gold badges were escorting a handcuffed Juan to an unmarked car. The news reporter explained that the FBI had conducted a nearly two-year sting on an Austin drug ring and the sting came to a close as they arrested a local drug dealer.

When I saw him on the TV in handcuffs, I was terrified. Although I had been looking for ways to get out from under Juan's control, I was concerned about how I was going to pay for everything. He had been supporting me for two years, paying for my apartment and my car. I was his mistress. This brought me to my next concern—what if they connected me back to him? I was clearly associated with him. Would I go to jail too? Would they come to question me? I had never been involved in any of his drug deals, and I made sure to stay clear of his family since I was the "mistress ghost" to them. Yet I was still afraid.

I called my mother, hysterically crying, but she was ecstatic. "I've been praying him out of your life, Becky, since you were sixteen. God has answered my prayers!"

She immediately came over to my apartment with Crystaline to calm me down. She assured me that if I had no connection to his work or dealings, I would be fine. Thank God, I was. It was as though I didn't even exist in his life, which I was thankful for!

In the weeks that followed Juan's arrest, I finally had the breathing room to think about my life and the choices I had made. I was on a path of total failure and destruction: I had dropped out of high school, didn't have two pennies to rub together, and now I had a daughter who was nearly a year old that I didn't know. The only reason she was in my life was because of Mom's empathy and patience. My mother, the one who let me down growing up, had become the one and only person I could now count on, the person I couldn't be. She had taken care of Crystaline for her first year and kept her out of the foster care system.

My introspection didn't get any better. I had no education, no career, no money, no skills. All of my relationships were detrimental. Though I began to see how my choices were directly correlated to the cycle of bad decisions and bondage I was engaged in, I couldn't yet see a way out. I didn't know how to stop doing what I was doing.

So, I kept working as a cocktail waitress. This time around, though, since I no longer had my sugar daddy to pay for my rent and other bills, I began saving enough money to stay in my apartment and pay my own rent. Since I was a single mother, Mom helped me officially get on welfare for food stamps and WIC (Women, Infant, Children —a federally funded nutrition program) so I could help Mom buy grocery items like milk. I hated getting on welfare, but I knew I had to do what I had to do in order to survive. The day when I got on government assistance, I made a vow it would only be temporary and somehow, someway I would find a way to get off of it.

Slowly, as I began putting my life together, Mom began giving me short, supervised visits with Crystaline. She wouldn't leave her overnight with me, but it was a start. It was something. In that period, thanks to my mom, she and I started our journey of getting to know each other. Instead of cutting her off or cursing at her, I started talking *with* her. Here I was, a nineteen-year-old mom with a nearly one-year-old baby whom I hadn't raised, trying to open my heart and learn how to love.

Thankfully, Crystaline was a good baby and rarely cried. She smiled a lot, and every time she was in a room, she drew attention; she looked like a little doll. People constantly asked about her name and age. She also started sitting on my lap for longer periods of time and staying for afternoon visits with me. It felt good to be loved, and that she did. Crystaline didn't see my faults, mistakes, or lack of anything; she just loved me.

Little did I know that in just a couple of weeks, my life would be forever transformed.

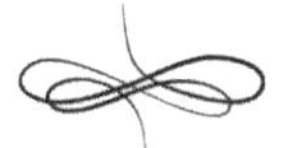

"If you don't address the wounds of your past, you will continue to bleed in your future."

—IYANLA VANZANT

CHAPTER THREE

EMBRACING MY TRANSFORMATION

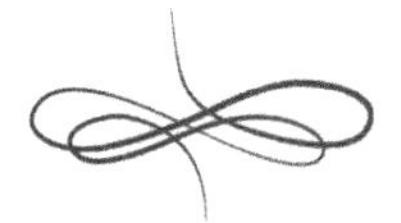

"Your present circumstances don't determine where you can go; they merely determine where you start."

—NIDO QUBEIN

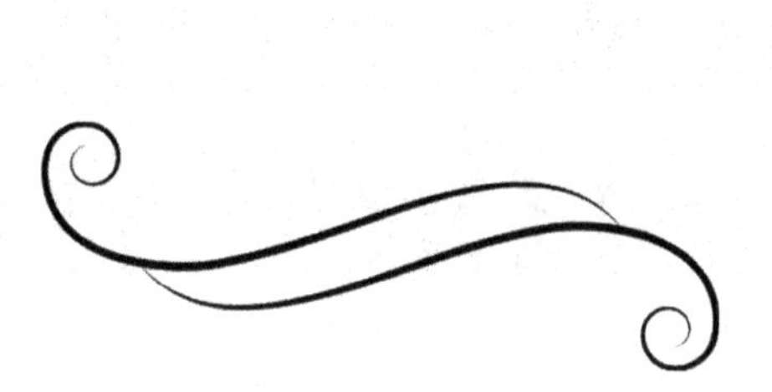

Church was the last place I wanted to be. Based on my experience, it offered nothing but negativity, judgment, and legalistic pastors like Grandpa Willie. Of course, his was the only church I knew, so I had nothing to compare it to. For me, all churches were the same, with a tyrannical God crammed down the throats of those who dared to enter. It was the only God I had ever known, the same rule-bound and suffocating God Grandpa Willie preached about in his church. Whoever or whatever it was, it had failed me. It kept my mother, my siblings, and me under the thumb of a narcissist abusive grandfather. It was a God I wanted nothing to do with. And I'm pretty sure that after Grandma Hope found Mom in Woolworth's, it was the same God that Grandma Keta was referring to when she said, "This God situation, I don't care about."

Despite my disdain for religion and my attraction to a wayward teen lifestyle, Mom never gave up on me. She had been inviting me to church for years and kept praying and asking and hoping. She would admit, "Becky, I know I've failed you, but God will never fail you. I know you don't want anything to do with God or with me, and you have good reason, but I want you to know that I believe God is going to work a miracle in your life." She truly lived it, declared it regularly, and believed it deep in her soul.

Mom had become a different mother than the one I had grown up with. From my perspective, three major life events transformed her. The first was her miraculous delivery from a ten-year addiction to drugs and alcohol. She replaced it with her newfound passion for serving God and the drug addict and her true heart for the homeless and the down-and-out. She knew what it was like to live on the streets and struggle with addictions. As an adult, it was not uncommon for me to visit Mom and find a drunk homeless person sleeping on our couch or a sick person she was nursing back to health or meet a young single mom she had taken in and then later, taken to Goodwill to buy them clothes. Even though she herself was poor, she always gave what little she had.

I'd warn, "Mom, you can't keep bringing homeless people into your house. You don't know what mental illness they struggle with, and you're not safe."

She'd smile. "I can help them, so I'm going to." She had a heart as big as Texas.

The second major life event for Mom was leaving Grandpa Willie—his church, his home, his rules, and his way of doing things. She had finally gotten out of his grip, and it was the best thing that could have happened to her.

These changes took place just in time for her to embrace the third major life event—Crystaline's birth. With her newfound freedom, she could now be fully present and loving, not only as a grandma to Crystaline but also as a mother to me. Even when I was rude or cursed her out, she remained steadfast in her patience with me and in her resolve to see me change. Mom would tell me and her friends, "I have hope that God will reach my kids, no matter what they're doing or what bad behaviors they're engaging in." She relentlessly prayed for us even though we had decided not to follow her God.

This irritated me a lot at the time. I didn't want her help, her hope. I was thankful she took care of my daughter, but I still harbored deep resentment and downright hate in my heart toward her personally. She had failed me as a mother. Why did I need her counsel now at age eighteen? No thank you! Nonetheless, about once or twice a month, every holiday, and for various church events, she continued to ask me to go to church with her at Templo Sinai.

I always had "reasons" to reject her offers. The services just didn't fit in with my party schedule—Sunday and Wednesday night services conflicted with ladies' night at the club, and Sunday morning services were impossible after pulling an all-nighter. To be truthful, I simply had no interest in stepping foot in any church… ever. Too many bad memories and no interest in revisiting them.

After Juan's abrupt arrest, Mom approached me again. "Becky, will you come to church with me Thursday night? I am visiting another church called Jubilee in North Austin as they have a special speaker and special music this week, and it's not going to be a traditional service. I think you'll have a good time. If you still want to leave after an hour, then you can leave. Just please come with me for a little while."

She finally wore me down. "All right," I relented. "I'll go with you this one time. But listen, this is the last time I want you to talk to me about your God. I don't ever want to hear about it again. I'm going with you just to shut you up."

She agreed to my terms. Her huge smile and the excitement in her eyes told me that she remained hopeful.

A LIFE-ALTERING MOMENT

Thursday night, I donned a short skirt and tank top and applied heavier makeup for the club's lighting. First, I had to endure one hour with mom at the church she was visiting, but then I'd leave at 8:30 p.m. to meet my friends for another night of fun. One of them needed a ride, so I convinced her to come with me to the service so I wouldn't have to go back and get her.

Earlier that night, Mom had asked me to keep my heart open. She knew I had a bad taste in my mouth for religion and ministers, and I was prepared to be critical of both that night. So I walked into that church expecting what I had always known—a stifling, brow-beating atmosphere. This time, however, it felt different—warm and peaceful. I settled into a seat in the back row, captivated by the beautiful and joyful voice of a woman singing at the front of the sanctuary. Her melodic tone and the music that accompanied it made me feel safe.

People stood, wearing huge smiles and obviously enjoying themselves. The pastor, Jimmy, greeted everyone from the pulpit. His voice, his smile, and relaxed body language spoke kindness, love, and a sincere welcome. After Jimmy introduced him, the visiting preacher gave his sermon. I kept waiting for him to start yelling and forcing people to deal with their sin, but it never happened.

I began to feel an emptiness in my heart that I can only describe as a big black hole. I reflected on my life and the mistakes of my past as well as the direction I was headed. I didn't know how to change. Softly, inside my heart, I confessed, "Here I am, nineteen years old, a high school dropout. I don't have two pennies to rub together. I have a daughter who doesn't know me, who's growing up without a father or a mother. What am I doing? I've made some bad choices, and I want out."

About thirty minutes later, the preacher made an altar call asking people from age eighteen to twenty-one to come up for prayer. Apparently, due to the sheer crowd size, each night he called a specific age group up. He indicated it was a night of receiving a miracle.

I glanced around to see what others were doing. My mother rose and joined that line of young adults to "stand in my stead." She turned back to me, her eyes pleading to join her. She later told me that while in that prayer line, she silently prayed, "God, please help my daughter. She's here, and I don't know when she'll come to church with me again, so please reach her where she is. Show her that You love her and that You are a real God. Please let her open her heart to change."

With drugs in my purse, ready for a night out, I felt incredibly compelled to pray. I silently said, "God, if You are real, help me. I need help. I can't do this alone. I want You to change my life."

Within seconds, God showed up. I had what I can only describe as a supernatural encounter with Him. It was a crystal clear demonstration of His love for me for the first time in my life. It felt like a warm blanket covering my soul as it filled in those deep trenches dug by rejections in my past. It was an experience that's difficult to explain to someone who has never shared it.

My perspective changed in an instant. My life flashed before me, all the way to my current circumstances with nowhere to go but up. I realized that God had heard me just then and heard my mother's prayers for the last several years. I felt a miracle transpiring in my own life. I cried out, overwhelmed by what I was feeling. "God, you know me. You know what I've done. You know how I've lived my life, how I've cursed You. Why would You care to reach me and touch my heart?"

His presence intensified, and I was overwhelmed by an even greater love than I felt moments earlier. I had nothing to offer God in return—in fact my life was a complete mess—but I wanted to be healed; I wanted to be forgiven. I was tired of feeling hopeless, tired of being angry, and tired of feeling hate toward those in my life who had taken advantage of me or abused me. I was just tired of life as it was. I silently prayed a simple but powerful prayer: "I've made a mess of my life. I'm a complete and total loser. I don't know what You can do with me, but I surrender all that I am to You, Jesus. Forgive me, help me, and heal me. I want a better life for my daughter."

My mother saw me break down in tears. She knew she was witnessing the miracle that she had been hoping and praying for all these years. Everyone saw her kick her shoes off and leap for joy again and again, lifting her three hundred pounds into the air as if she were light as a feather. She kept yelling out, "Thank you, God! Thank you, Jesus! Thank you for reaching my daughter." Tears streamed down her face for all to see, but she didn't care and neither did I. That night for the first time in my entire life, when I looked at my mom, all I could do was smile.

My friend was freaked out, she didn't understand what was taking place. She had to find another ride to the club because I didn't go. Instead, I followed Mom home in my car. I needed to talk with her about my experience as well as figure out our path forward as a family.

After Mom put Crystaline to bed that night, she walked into her little kitchen where I sat in shock, still emotional from my encounter with God and overall experience. Her face still wore that huge smile. She wrapped her arms around me, and I embraced her in return. We cried together for what seemed like hours, although it was only about thirty minutes.

She said, "*Mija* ["daughter" in Spanish], I love you so much. I know this is going to be hard, but I'm going to help you. Trust me and trust God. We're all doing this together." She understood firsthand that the road before me was beyond tough in many ways. Neither of us could have known all that lay ahead for this impoverished high school dropout with addiction issues and a heart filled with unforgiveness, resentment, and emotional dysfunction. It would take years to work through it all. But the good news was that the healing process had already begun, a step in the right direction for me.

That night I embraced two of the most important relationships I would need to make change happen. One required restoration with Mom and learning to trust her while the other provided the excitement of a new relationship with the real God, not some religious zealot who wanted to send me to hell or strike me dead when I made mistakes. This God truly loved me just as I was yet loved me enough to not leave me the same.

I had hit my rock bottom just like my mother had. Enough was enough. I was ready to surrender and begin the learning and transformation process, a long journey up and into a better life.

That next night I went back to church with Mom and this time brought Earl with me. He was my party partner. I loved my twin brother deeply and knew he needed to change just as much as I did. The fact is that Mom had been praying for both of us, never giving up hope that together we would experience much needed transformation in our lives. Earl's conversion started not too long after mine.

NEW BEGINNINGS

Within weeks, I learned that healing and restoration weren't going to be easy, so I quit my job at the bar and moved back in with Mom. It wasn't what I wanted to do, but it was what I needed to do. I'd spent the last several years without rules or boundaries. But something special had happened to me and I was just at the beginning of having to deal with the mistakes and issues of my addictions, so I couldn't risk slipping back into my old life in a moment of weakness.

It was a tough move. Although I had started opening up to Mom, I still didn't like her very much. I still struggled to reconcile her intense faith with the poor choices she'd made early on in my life. In many ways, her religion and heavy hand were what drove me to rebel in the first place, and I had to come to terms with that as I began my faith journey.

I eventually came to believe that she had my best interests at heart. But we had so much baggage in our history, and frankly we just didn't get along. We were oil and water. Mom had deep-seated bad behaviors that stemmed from her past and upbringing, and she was too stubborn to change them. Even in her faith, the bad behaviors followed her. For example, she never held down a job. She relied on the welfare system or on other people to take care of her. I never understood or liked that.

I also needed to heal my relationship with my daughter and living in the same house with Crystaline allowed her to get to know me better and allowed me to be a hands-on mother. She was already thirteen months old, and I had missed out on her entire first year, a critical age for mother-baby bonding. She had bonded with Mom and not with me, so I could rarely take her away from Mom without her crying. It put me at a tremendous disadvantage. Mom also didn't trust me to be alone with her until I could prove I had taken the necessary steps to change. Sound familiar? Regardless, we had made a start.

The next thing I did was cut off the toxic people in my life. For the most part, it happened naturally. We no longer had anything in common, so I found a new group of friends. I started attending Mom's church. She was very involved and taught in their Bible Institute. Mom told me the church had an amazing youth group with a great outreach program that included multiple community activities and weekly events and encouraged me to join in. I finally had those innocent experiences I was never allowed to enjoy as a child, simple things like eating out after church, picnics, field trips to the San Antonio Zoo, water balloon fights, volleyball tournaments at the lake, baseball games on a Saturday afternoon. It was a way for me to plug into a healthy, life-giving organization with other young people committed to growing in their faith.

I also got involved with a regimented Bible study program called the Fire Institute. It required its members to attend all church services, observe a 10:00 p.m. curfew, and refrain from one-on-one dating. Having structure in my life was a completely new experience but what I desperately needed at the time. Unlike Grandpa Willie's dictates and forced submissions, the program didn't emphasize heavy rules as much as it encouraged personal discipline and accountability.

But once alone back in my room, I grappled with all my past decisions and where they had gotten me. My body fought the physical and emotional effects of detoxification. Surprisingly, my mother, who never engaged in anything important with me growing up, became my biggest cheerleader and coach. She knew a thing or two about kicking addictions, making bad decisions with men, and transitioning from destructive behaviors to positive choices. She made it clear that she was going to be there for me now and in the future. Knowing all of this gave me comfort and strength to keep going.

Many nights, I would wake up from a nightmare in a cold sweat, ready to seek out any chemical to help me cope. But my mother was always right there to help me, pray with me, and nurture me through it. The first six months were the most challenging as I pressed through the urges to pick up the bottle again or revert to another feel-good night with a drug.

Mom made sure she kept me super busy with the youth group. Dave and Lupita, the youth pastor and his wife, were a Godsend to me. They knew my past and encouraged me every step of the way. Lupita modeled a deeply caring mom-like role and would come over and pray with me. She also paired me with a mentor, a young single woman who was strong in her faith. We met weekly to talk through my negative thoughts and urges and to pray. I now realize how similar this was to having an accountability buddy in AA who stands by you and walks with you through the difficult journey to become sober.

MY KNIGHT IN SHINING ARMOR

Mom also made sure I attended every church service with her. They were life-giving and fun, not boring and rule oriented. Back then, the church also held Saturday night youth services, and I attended them full of excitement. For that first event, Mom walked me to the youth building and started introducing me to people. My eyes fell on a handsome man playing the drums. I was captivated by his striking features and gorgeous black hair and the happiness that radiated from his smile and eyes. Although he was sitting on a stool, I could tell he was tall. And wow, did he seem passionate about his faith!

Mom noticed my gaze. "That's David, Becky, the man I've been telling you about. Your knight in shining armor."

I remembered quite well. She had gotten to know David in her role as a teacher in the Bible school. He was her student, taking numerous Bible courses as a volunteer in the youth ministry. She'd tell me how he was a talented drummer and a gifted playwright and director for the church plays. Connecting the dots, I finally realized she had been telling me about David since I was sixteen. After Juan was thrown into jail, she'd said, "I found a daddy for Crystaline."

Of course, back then, I had never met David, so I responded, "I'm not interested in a church boy, Mom. No thank you."

Fast forward to not-quite-nineteen years old in my newfound faith, and boy was I rethinking my words! As I got to know David, my new opinion of him only got better. During the young adults' classes on Sunday mornings, I sat in awe as I listened to him speak, his passion pouring out. I loved the way he taught and shared God's Word and his passion to serve and help people, in particular the youth. When I learned he had also struggled with addiction in the past, I felt a kindred spirit with him, knowing he too had walked that path to freedom just five years before me.

Not long after I joined the youth group, Mom's proclamation intensified. "Honey," she said, "I just know that David is Crystaline's daddy and your husband. I'm going to pray for God to bring you together."

I laughed. "Mom, please! My focus should be on my transformation and relationship with God and getting to know my daughter. The last thing I need right now is a guy. Stand down and quit playing Cupid."

Earl had also started going to church with us and had his own transformation shortly after mine. He and mom often ganged up on me with the notion that David was "the one." Although I admired David (and as time went on, the admiration turned into more liking), I couldn't allow myself to be distracted from my goal of truly healing my life, dealing with my past, and getting on the right track. I had to remain 100 percent focused. Plus, David was a volunteer youth leader in the church, and a *near-perfect* guy! There was no way someone like him would ever be interested in someone like me, with my past and baggage.

Nonetheless, Mom and Earl both prayed regularly and would tell me they were asking God to make a way for David and me to get together, that Crystaline would have David as her father. And once Mama went to praying—well, it was all over. Her faith remained rock solid. She never stopped believing we would be together, and she never stopped reminding me. She loved David for me before we had ever met. After months of hearing them declare this request before God, I joined them. I was determined to ensure that, unlike me, my daughter would grow up with a father in her life. So, I began my personal intimate petition to God to bring us together as a family.

MY NEW BEST FRIEND

In 1989, David was involved in inner-city outreach working with underprivileged youth and local gangs. In particular, he and the youth pastor, Dave, were both very engaged in an outreach in Austin where we held assemblies and hosted after-school clubs. We performed several of David's plays in the local Austin high schools.

David was the real deal and not there for show. He was a "roll up your sleeves and help" type of person, determined to make a difference, to improve the lives of these young people. But at that time, I didn't realize his passion came from his own experience of transformation just five years before I met him.

Back then, East Austin had a huge problem with weekend shootings between three major gangs. Once the youth pastor and his right-hand volunteer, David, got wind of this problem, David came up with a solution. He knew these young men liked three things—baseball, BBQ, and competition. On a Saturday morning, he drove to their neighborhood, found out where they hung out, and boldly challenged one of the gangs to a game of softball. He proposed, "If we win, you have to come to a youth service at our church. If you win, then we will cook out and have a barbecue on a day of your choosing, you can bring your families out, and we'll feed all of them."

They accepted the challenge, and each of the other gangs decided to do so as well. The competitions would be played on consecutive Saturday mornings, with each game involving a different gang. After the second game, the Austin Police Department (APD) showed up at our church office asking for David Contreras. David met them with Pastor Dave by his side. The police had heard that David and Dave had gotten the gangs to play softball. "How are you doing it?" they asked. "We want to help." Consequently, the APD supervised the last softball game played at a large baseball park.

David and the church youth team won the game, but the big win was getting the three major gang leaders to show up to the PowerSource youth ministry gathering one Saturday night. It was a sight to see!

One of David's original plays, *Man in the Mirror*, depicted gang life and its tragic consequences. All three gangs sat under one church roof, watching their lives unfold through David's play. I knew these gang members and leaders from my past life, as we were all about the same age and grew up in East Austin. They lived in my neighborhood, and we attended middle school together. Now here we all were, coming together in God's house!

The APD observed this spectacular event, with officers standing against the walls inside that small chapel, in awe. Shortly afterward, the APD commander asked David if he would support them in helping bring the three main gang leaders together to sign a two-year truce. Because of Pastor Dave and David's instrumental leadership and outreach, they got to witness this significant reformation and see the gang shootings stop in East Austin for two solid years.

During that period, my friendship with David blossomed. It was the first healthy relationship I'd ever had with a male, and he was my first healthy male role model. He made me feel safe, secure, respected, and genuinely cared for. It was purely friendship, and I loved the fact that we could talk, laugh, and have things in common with no expectations.

Mom encouraged my relationship with David and frequently took Crystaline so I could go out and have fun with him and some members of the youth group. Crystaline and I were still living with her, along with Amber and, at times, Earl. He and David ended up becoming good friends. Daniel had married young and started a family.

In those eighteen months of knowing David, he gradually became my best friend. We had so much in common, not only our past challenges with drugs and alcohol, but also our big dreams for our future. Then the butterfly flutters started happening every time I saw him or heard his name—I was beginning to fall in love with him. David, however, wanted to help me get my life back on track. He understood I'd had bad experiences with men in the past, and he said he never wanted to be a stumbling block in my personal growth.

David was quite the gentleman, and he never so much as held my hand during the first year I knew him.

GETTING OFF WELFARE, ABANDONING POVERTY

My newfound internal freedom gave me permission to dream. The possibility of obtaining the impossible and my growing relationship with God became the crux of my life. For so many years, I had been following in my mother's footsteps, making all the same bad mistakes she had, the same ones I had hated her for. Now I realized I could create my own path and form my own footsteps for the sake of Crystaline. I fervently pursued change.

In the fall of 1989, within months of my encounter with God, I took the next step in my personal transformation by enrolling in the state-funded Welfare-to-Work Program through the Job Training Partnership Act (JTPA). It was designed to get single moms off welfare and into viable jobs. These employments were only temporary—three to six months—but they introduced these moms, particularly high school dropouts, to new opportunities they might have never had otherwise. It was up to them to get hired permanently at the end of the six-month term.

I applied to the program and received a full sponsorship, acquired my GED, and graduated from the program in six weeks. In October 1989, there was a receptionist position available in the State Treasury Department under Ann Richards, the elected state treasurer. She wanted to hire a JTPA program graduate through a competitive application process.

Ten graduates applied, and I was one of three chosen for an interview. I really wanted that job! Not only did I need the money, but it was my chance to raise my daughter in a stable life that didn't involve the welfare system. Plus, it was a fantastic opportunity to work in the Texas state government!

Imagine my surprise when I was hired. The HR director told me I stood out in my interview because I seemed "hungrier" and more eager to learn. She couldn't have been more accurate. To say I was excited is an understatement! I had a job with Treasurer Ann Richards, an extraordinary figure to me as a young Latina who was trying to work herself out of poverty. The more I got to see her in action, the more impressive the thought of being a female leader someday became. It was the first time I had seen a woman in a position of power.

Her heart for helping and empowering women in particular was sincere. She was a truly kind person. Whenever she came into the office, she made a point to stop and talk to me and to take an interest in my life. I was desperate to prove myself in my job to a new boss and to the treasurer of the state, Ms. Richards, or just Ann, as she liked to be called.

I worked hard, probably more than was expected from my position. But I soon found out that I thrived on the challenges that came my way, whether they were mine in the first place or my colleagues'. They frequently brought their problematic work issues to me, and I accepted them and ran with them, excited to learn and honored by their trust in me. More and more coworkers began to say, "If you need something done and done right, get Rebecca to do it." I was building a new reputation, earning respect and comradery.

It didn't take long to realize that being a receptionist for the treasurer of the state of Texas offered more than a steady paycheck. Working in the front office taught me the ins and outs of working for a state official. It was a life-changing event that put me on the course to a successful career.

LET THE DATING BEGIN

My eyes were being opened to different types of people both professionally and personally. The more I learned about David and got to know him, the more I realized he was exactly the kind of person I wanted as a father for Crystaline. Of course, early on, I kept those thoughts and emotions to myself; I didn't want to scare him away. I did discuss this with both my mother and brother as they were both huge "David fans" and knew a relationship with him was in my future.

I quit laughing at them or telling them that marrying someone like David was a pipe dream. Instead, I prayed along with them that he would marry me. All three of us intently prayed David into the family. Still, deep down inside, my shame, insecurity, and lack of self-worth kept trying to convince me that I didn't deserve someone like him.

David was such a good person. Every young single woman (and perhaps older too) wanted to marry him. No joke. He had a line of women waiting in the wings who were praying for him to be their husband.

Within months of arriving at that church, several young ladies in their twenties informed me that David would not be interested in me due to my past. They told me they had been serving God their whole life, had kept themselves pure, and deserved him more than me. Their self-righteous attitudes reminded me of Grandpa Willie, and it turned me off from them. I cut the cord with that group of young women and moved on to other friends who truly had my best interests at heart, saw my value, and wanted to see me grow, learn, and advance. In the end, though, their negative words ran over and over in my mind. I couldn't argue with them. Why would David be interested in me, I had nothing to offer except the baggage of my past? However, I couldn't deny that we had a magnetic attraction when we were together. We laughed a lot together, really enjoyed each other's company as friends, and we could talk for hours on end about our goals and our individual dreams.

Then one day, after eighteen months of friendship, it happened—David asked me out on a date. He said he had feelings for me and wanted to see where it would lead.

Because we were such good friends, I felt comfortable laying out my expectations. I said, "I don't want to be in a relationship just for fun. I have a daughter, and anyone I date needs to be sure he can be her father because I don't have time to mess around with a relationship going nowhere. Crystaline needs a daddy."

He patiently listened. "Rebecca," he responded. "I deeply care for you. I've started to get to know Crystaline. I want you to give me a chance. Let's just start dating and see where it leads."

We started officially dating in November of 1989. Shortly afterward, we performed one of David's plays at a Corpus Christi youth convention with over five hundred young people. He played the lead character, and he had cast me as his girlfriend. We began to view ourselves together in a way we had not yet experienced. The play turned out to be a big hit, and we returned home to Austin officially boyfriend-girlfriend.

Then, the week before Christmas 1989, just one month after our first date and two months after I started my job at the Treasury Department, David proposed to me. We set our wedding date for four months later, in April of 1990. It was that fast. We had been such good friends for so long, and we knew what we wanted in life.

With no time to mess around, we jumped in fully—hook, line, and sinker!

MY CAREER ON THE MOVE

My life was more than I could have asked for. I was engaged to the love of my life, and I loved working for the treasury. They treated me well, and I was finally finding value in myself. Also, Ann Richards had started her run for governor, which made my job in the front executive office more exciting as we supported the iconic Texas official.

My three-month temporary position with the state was coming to end. When a full-time permanent position opened up supporting the human resources (HR) director, I immediately applied. While waiting for my interview in the office, a nicely dressed gentleman struck up a conversation with me, asking about my background and why I was there. I later learned that he was Ann's budget director. After we talked, he went right into the HR director's office and said, "You need to hire that young lady outside." He later told me that there was something about me, that I seemed to really want the job, and he liked the fact that I was a single mom trying to get my life straightened out.

I took his endorsement as one more sign that tremendous favor was upon me. I was hired right away, taken from temporary to full-time government employee. For the first time in my life, I had a good job with good benefits for Crystaline and me. I could now get off welfare and begin my journey to support my daughter. It didn't matter that I was starting at ground zero. I had so much to learn and so far to go, but I was all in. I had made it!

HERE COMES THE BRIDE

God had answered our prayers. Four months after David and I were engaged, on April 7, 1990, I walked down the aisle to marry the man of my dreams.

I was just twenty-one, and Crystaline was three. David was thirty-one, and neither of us had any money. I was employed in an entry-level government job, and David earned an hourly wage working in a political campaign for a man running for Austin City Council. Yet, we considered ourselves blessed. Somehow God provided.

Many people came out of the woodwork to donate support for our expenses for that exceptional day. We lacked nothing and had a beautiful, large wedding, and we didn't go into debt to pay for it. Ours was a Cinderella story, and many wanted to get behind it and be a part of it.

David also somehow arranged for a limo and driver to be donated. It picked me up from the new apartment he had rented for us about a week beforehand so that everything would be ready when we moved into it after the wedding. To make the event more special, my brother Daniel, now home from the Marine Corps, gave me away in full uniform. Earl was in the wedding party and spoke at the reception. Amber, then thirteen, came with Mom. She and Grandma Keta sat in one church sharing the joyous occasion together.

It was a magical day for me. I felt like a princess out of a fairytale and looked like one too. Bear in mind, this dream of marrying a good man in wedding attire was one I never thought would happen. My mother was briefly married, and that was only to give us a last name, and my grandmother was never married. Healthy marriages with full-on weddings were not a family tradition.

David and I honeymooned in Puerto Vallarta, Mexico (a gift from David's mother and my first time ever to board an airplane) while Crystaline stayed with Mom. When we returned, we moved into our own little apartment—just David, me, and Crystaline. We were a family. It was a dream come true. But it was a dream we would wake up from quickly.

JUAN RETURNS

Two months into our marriage, a ghost from my past suddenly appeared at the State Treasury Department. I walked outside to wait for David to pick me up after work. As my eyes scanned the parking lot for David's car, I froze. Leaning against a dark sports car with arms folded over his chest was Juan. His smirk pronounced, "I own you."

Fear ran through my body as I tried to control the shaking. *Why?* I wondered. *Why is he not in prison? It's only been two years since he was locked away.* I composed myself enough to rush back inside to wait for David there. Within the safety of the building, I peered through the glass door just in time to see Juan speeding off. He probably assumed I went in to call the cops or ask someone to help.

In the prior two years, I had dealt with many deep-rooted issues and things about my past, but Juan wasn't one of them, his memory I buried deep. I was happy to simply move on with my life without him in it and act like he had never existed. While I had worked on forgetting about him, though, he clearly had not forgotten about me. The last thing I expected was for him to return, but return he did. (I later learned he had been released from prison early on a technicality.) I was now forced to pull up those suppressed memories.

Of course, David knew about Juan. Well, some things. He knew that Juan was Crystaline's biological dad and that he was my ex, a drug dealer I had gotten involved with early on in my teen life. He didn't know the extent of the control Juan had over me or about the abuse I had sustained from him. He didn't know that Juan had tried to murder me and violently raped me. I had never told anyone about my abusive relationship with Juan, nor did I want to dredge it up. In trying to block these things out of my own mind, I had blocked them out for David too. The last thing I wanted to do was tell David about that part of my past, but I could no longer keep it from him.

That night after dinner, I told David how Juan showed up at my job, and then I told him the rest of my story. The next morning, Juan called my office and insisted on seeing me. I asked him for his number and told him I would have David call him.

The number Juan gave me turned out to be a general number for where he worked. David drove to his job.

When he arrived, Juan refused to come out and sent his boss to talk to David instead. His boss told David that Juan was on parole, didn't want any trouble, and, according to him, was just trying to see his daughter. David said, "Under no circumstances is Juan to call Rebecca or go by her job again if he wants to see his daughter. I'm happy to arrange a meeting to talk with him man-to-man and make arrangements, but I will remind you and Juan that Rebecca is no longer single. She is now my wife, and Crystaline is my daughter by marriage. If Juan wants to see Crystaline, he can meet me as Rebecca's husband and work out the terms, but it's not going to happen without me involved." David never flinched, never showed any fear as he matter-of-factly laid down the terms.

We attended church that following Sunday night. As we were walking out of the building afterwards, I spotted a dark sports car near the entrance with its motor running. The driver's side was facing us, and the window was rolled down, giving me an unobstructed view of its driver—Juan. I froze in mid-stride.

David looked at me, his eyes questioning. Seeing my ashen face and trembling body, his eyes followed mine. "That's Juan," I managed to whisper.

David looked at me and then again at Juan. "Take Crystaline, and go back inside," he instructed. He then calmly walked over to Juan's car door and bent at the waist to talk to him through his window.

Juan claimed, "I'm only here to see my daughter."

David responded, "Juan, if you want to see your daughter, and if you want to talk about terms, about what that's going to look like, I'll sit down and talk to you. I'm a reasonable person. But you're not going to go through my wife. You're going to go through me."

Juan stared toward the church doors for a few moments, contemplating David's words. Then he shrugged and nodded. "Okay. I can do that."

David retrieved an old business card from his pocket and wrote down a date, time, and address of where they would meet. Juan took the card and glanced back at the church doors hiding Crystaline and me one last time before driving off.

I was terrified for Juan to see Crystaline. "David," I said, "I don't want him to have anything to do with me or her. Deep in my gut, I know it's me he wants, and he'll do anything or say anything to get to me."

David wrapped his arms around me to assure me. "It's just going to be a first meeting. I'm going to hear him out to see if he's serious. If he is, then you and I together will discuss the path forward and the right thing for Crystaline. Don't worry. I won't allow Juan near you or Crystaline, and I won't make any irrational decisions without your agreement."

I nodded in understanding and was thankful.

That next week, David arrived at the appointed time for his meeting with Juan. He waited and waited, but Juan never showed up. He wasn't serious about seeing his daughter; he just wanted to get at me, and he didn't want to deal with David to do it.

David and I agreed then and there that we would never allow Juan near Crystaline. Juan, however, wasn't part of that agreement. He wasn't done.

MY ALL-IN COACH FOR SUCCESS

I had been at the State Treasury Department for over a year when Ann was elected governor in 1991, and her team left to work at the State Capitol. I stayed where I was, and in came the new state treasurer, Kay Bailey Hutchison. She placed very smart women on her leadership team, and I studied them all to learn all I could in order to grow in my career.

One such team leader was Donna. She became the new HR director. Besides her professional acuity and expertise in human resources, the woman behind the title turned out to be the kindest, most patient person I had ever met. She recognized my eagerness to learn and continually encouraged me, saying, "Rebecca, you have potential." Taking me under her wing, she invested in me, believing that equipping me with the right knowledge and skills was essential to my success. She enrolled me in a professional class at least once a month to ensure I had additional training in communications, leadership, conflict resolution, writing, and more—all the fundamentals needed to grow and succeed. Having grown up in the hood with little focus on my education, my English and communication skills were miserable, and my vocabulary included regularly used street slang. One of the first two classes she sent me to was focused on communication and dressing for success. She was determined to put me on a track to become a supervisor.

Donna was also a mom and wife. She knew my history and became the role model I had never had. Her interest in learning more about my extended family and David and Crystaline enabled me to open up and share some of the struggles I was having as a new wife and mother. She counseled me for hours each week, and over time we developed a very close friendship. Donna became my "all-in" coach and my first dedicated mentor.

Donna was a game-changer in my life and growth. I am forever grateful to her and many others along the way for seeing my potential and giving me a chance to prove myself. But at that time, I don't think any of us knew just how far I would fly.

CHAPTER FOUR

THE MOSAIC OF nEW LIFE

"The most important thing is not your start in life but how you navigate the journey and create the mosaic of your future."

—REBECCA CONTRERAS

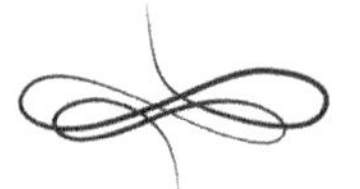

The threat to our family continued to lurk, yet neither David nor I could see it. It was out of sight, out of mind, and the false security that goes along with it. That was until it almost crashed into me.

About a year after we were married, I was driving to Crystaline's day care to pick her up after work. Glancing in my rearview mirror, I saw a car approaching way too fast. Then it started tailgating me and tried to run me off the road. As I braced myself for a rear-end collision, it swerved, barely missing the rear corner of my vehicle, and drove up alongside me.

It didn't pass, just kept the same speed as me. Feeling like I was being watched, I glanced over and got a glimpse of the maniac driving it. My heart raced when I saw that it was Juan. He had come for me again! This time I was all alone.

He motioned for me to pull over. I complied, hoping I could calm him down and prevent an accident. He pulled behind me and rushed to my vehicle. I thought, *What does he want now? Didn't David make the terms clear enough to him? Yet here he is. Why can't he just leave me alone?*

It all happened so fast. Before I could lock the doors, he climbed into the passenger seat of my car. "You didn't write to me in prison, Becky." His tone was calm, too calm.

I had no idea what he was going to do; I had no idea what I was going to do. Taking a deep breath, I tried to keep fear out of my voice as I spoke. "Juan, we ended a long time ago. It's over. I'm married now. I have a family. I need you to leave me alone."

Juan grabbed my shoulders and pulled me to face him. "I'm taking Crystaline out of the state, and you'll never see her again," he threatened, his tone now menacing. "And David, your husband, well, I'm going to kill him, and you know I can. How would you like that? You'll be left all alone."

I knew I had to deescalate this and fast. I had to somehow calm him down. "Juan, listen. I'll talk to David again. We'll figure out a way for you to see Crystaline. Please, Juan, just let me go. She's waiting for me to pick her up."

He ignored my pleas and talked to me for what felt like hours. He bragged about his time in prison and what he was doing now, all the people he was involved with. The entire conversation was a blur, and I blocked him out. I kept thinking about how late it was getting, that I needed to get Crystaline, and how worried David was going to be because I wasn't home. But I couldn't share any of my thoughts and concerns with Juan; he didn't care.

I finally spoke again. "Juan, I'll do my best to convince David to agree to meet with you, and you can see Crystaline."

By some miracle, he let me go and left. The sound of his screeching car speeding off was beautiful music to my ears. I sat there for a moment before I allowed myself to break down and bawl; I was so terrified.

Knowing Juan was quite capable of doing what he threatened, I drove as fast as I could to Crystaline's day care, praying the whole way and thanking God for His protection over us. I didn't have a cell phone to call and warn them.

Thankfully, Crystaline was fine. I put her in my back seat. During the forty-five-minute drive home, I often glanced in my rearview mirror at her precious happy face. *How am I going to protect her from this man? What if she wants to see him when she gets older? How am I going to explain what happened today to David?* The unanswered questions and mistakes not dealt with from my past haunted me, threatening my peace and new life. I deeply regretted not having fully disclosed to David the abuse I had suffered at the hands of this horrible man.

David was a street fighter back in his pre-God days. He wasn't known for backing away from any threat or fight. I knew his personal journey and story; he was very vocal and proud of it. Although I was grateful for his protectiveness over Crystaline and me, I was also concerned that this incident would send him into a tailspin.

When I pulled into my driveway two hours later than normal, David greeted me with a furrowed brow and set jaw. He had been worried. He'd already called some of our friends, and they were all equally concerned. He had called the day care, and they told him I was very late in picking up Crystaline, so he knew something had happened.

As soon as I got her settled into her room to play and watch cartoons, I closed the door and collapsed on the couch in tears. As I told him what happened, including Juan's threat to kill him and take Crystaline, his worry turned to anger.

"Why did you pull over, Rebecca? Why did you even talk to him?"

I was so shaken and emotionally exhausted from the incident that I curled into a ball on the couch and began to shake and cry uncontrollably. I couldn't talk anymore.

David's anger just exacerbated things, but I could tell he was trying hard to understand the incident and how I got there. I tried to explain the events to him, but my sobs increased in frequency and duration. It just became hard for me to talk.

He studied me for a few moments, and then his narrowed eyes softened as his anger turned to compassion. He held me and told me everything was going to be okay. It took about an hour, but he calmed me down. Within his arms, I felt so secure and protected.

David was not going to let him bully me or us, and we couldn't let Juan continue to interfere in our lives. The next morning, we knew we had to address this incident now, but we had to think through how best to do it.

It didn't take long before we were forced to confront it head-on. Within two hours of dropping Crystaline off at her preschool, the administrator there called me at work, whispering into the phone. "The man you gave me a description of—he's here in the office. He's got a long scar across his neck just like you said, and he wants to see Crystaline. He claims he's her father."

I immediately called David at his job, which was about five minutes from the school. He then called the administrator and instructed her to call the police. "I'm on the way," he told her. Thankfully, he was a man of action and no fear.

I couldn't do anything but take a break from work, pace the restroom floor, and pray the encounter between David and Juan went well. Neither of them would back down, but I felt a sense of calm and peace with David by my side. I had married a fighter, a protector, and a man of great resolve. God forbid Juan tried to step in and take us away or hurt us!

When he arrived at the school, one of the staff told David, "He's waiting in the conference room for Mrs. Contreras."

When David entered the room, Juan was sitting at the table facing the door with a smirk on his face. But his expression turned to confusion when David closed the door behind him, signaling he was alone. Juan stared at David with intense hatred. Perhaps by then he knew he had lost. David put his palms on the table, leaned toward Juan, looked him in the eyes, and in a firm voice said, "You are not welcome in Rebecca's life or in Crystaline's life."

Juan shrugged. "I had her before you did, dude."

David replied, "All you have is a fading memory. Stay away from my family."

The police arrived. With Juan's prior record and David's testimony, there was no doubt that Juan didn't belong there, so they arrested him for trespassing. The incident got us a two-year restraining order against him, and thankfully, it worked. He stayed away from us.

A few years later, we received a call from a man in Austin. His daughter Becky and Juan had a little girl together. He said Juan had been physically and sexually abusing his grandchild, who was now three years old. He was forcing his daughter to take Juan to court for both the physical abuse charges on her and the sexual abuse of their daughter. They found out about me because Becky told her dad that Juan bragged about having another daughter with someone else also named Becky.

Her father pleaded with David to have me consider testifying about my history of abuse with Juan. I didn't want anything to do with Juan or this trial, but I also couldn't sit back and allow an innocent child to be abused. I reluctantly agreed.

David told the man, "She'll testify if you need her testimony to convict him." In the end, thank God, they had enough evidence without my testimony, so I didn't have to face him in court. Juan was sent back to prison.

That encounter gave me a glimpse of what my life might have been if I had stayed with Juan. The little girl might easily have been my Crystaline. I overflowed with gratitude for my mother, who helped me make a clean break from Juan after he first went to prison, and for David, my man of action who was willing to stand up to Juan and protect his young family.

We never saw Juan again. In 2012, we learned that he had been shot four times and killed in an altercation with a corrections officer after being rereleased from prison. Sadly, Juan's oldest son, who was about Crystaline's age, witnessed it.

Finally, my relief was complete. I would never wish death on anyone, but this man had done so many horrible things to hurt so many lives. I no longer had to carry the worry that Juan would return one day to hurt me, David, or Crystaline. I was free of him forever.

MY MARRIAGE ON THE ROCKS

For some women, being a good mother and wife seem to come naturally. Not for me. I had to work overtime at both, and I really didn't know what I was doing. Before Donna's mentorship, all my role models except my Grandma Keta had exemplified poor decisions and abuse. Grandma Keta had been out of my life for a while because she lived about twelve hours away in El Paso, so I only saw her for holidays on occasion. So what I had witnessed and experienced in terms of knowledge or learning how to be a mom or wife over the last ten years was all I had to go by.

I also still carried the shame of not being good enough for David. It didn't help that some in his family were not crazy about him marrying me with the baggage of bringing along an instant family. Several of those self-righteous girls in the church had apparently paid his mom and family a visit a few weeks before we got married to share all my past issues with his mother and siblings. They said, "David is making a big mistake marrying her." As a result, David's older brother, slotted to be his best man, dropped out of our wedding just weeks before the event. Thankfully, his mother, Jaine, was on my side from day one. She didn't care about my past and looked beyond it. She knew her son loved me and was happy, so that was enough for her. And when she met Crystaline, his mom fell in love with her right out of the gate. Janie had become like a mom to me, always loving and accepting me like her own daughter, and Crystaline like her own granddaughter.

David, on the other hand, brought his own baggage into the marriage that got mixed with mine. He had lost his father at age five. His mother was left to raise five young children alone (David is the middle child), and she fell into a deep depression. Although she worked hard and always provided a good home for them, because she held down two jobs at times, he had to fend for himself often. As a result of not having a father or anyone really present or engaged in his life, he struggled with drugs and anger issues that started in high school and spanned over a period of ten years.

When I met him, he was twenty-nine and had been drug-free for nearly six years, but once we got married, the deep-rooted anger still lingered and seeped into and throughout our early marriage. We loved each other very much, but we were not emotionally prepared to deal with the explosive issues of our past.

In the beginning, neither of us was aware of the ticking timebombs tucked away—my emotional dysfunction nor his anger. But we found out within weeks after giving our marriage vows. What had been repressed started creeping to the surface. Disagreements turned to arguments, which evolved into intense verbal fighting for days, and none of it led to any resolutions. Those first two years of our marriage were trial by fire.

Add to that my highly dysfunctional extended family, primarily Mom and Earl. David would have to deal with their issues that constantly seeped into our life together. I've always been the mama bear of the family, and when my mom or twin needed help, I'd feel compelled to rescue them. David would often say, "I didn't marry your mom or twin; I married you." And he was right.

Anytime David said something the slightest bit negative to me, my insecurity sprang to life, and my emotions spiraled out of control. He was always direct when he spoke and had a definitive, powerful voice, and his tone seemed aggressive to me. Because I hadn't dealt with my abusive past, I didn't know how to handle it. At times, we had unhealthy arguments. Tensions would flare and escalate, so he'd want to leave the room to avoid more blowups, and I'd want to force him to stay and work it out. He'd say, "This is going nowhere, so I need to get some air," and I'd chase him out of the house and accuse him of abandoning me. "Just leave me," I'd yell. "Everyone else has. Why not you?"

Due to his anger and our emotional dysfunctions, sometimes I'd rock myself in the fetal position in a corner of our small apartment. David would stand over me perplexed, no doubt wondering, *What's wrong with her?* His wide eyes and raised eyebrows silently yelled, *Oh, my gosh! I married a crazy woman!* He had no idea how to deal with my emotional outbursts. At the same time, I had no idea how to deal with his anger issues. My insecure behaviors would activate his own trauma and anger issues, and he would often verbally fly off the handle.

Amidst all this, we were still working hard to be good parents. We didn't want Crystaline to grow up in a home where her parents were always fighting. We were still trying to be good Christians. We were still trying to serve the community. We still knew we were meant to be together. We still loved each other passionately. We just didn't know how to navigate the difficulties of marriage that we were starting to face. We didn't understand how our past selves and deep-rooted issues were clouding the way we saw and communicated with each other. We didn't know how to get off the merry-go-round of drama and dysfunction we had set into motion. It is often said that marriage can bring out the best or worst in you; for us it was both.

The change had to start with me—I had to get help. I began to pray in earnest for my family and my marriage. Then God brought to light the things I'd been keeping in the shadows, things I needed to examine and let go of before my personal healing could begin.

I also began seeking counsel from others in leadership roles I looked up to, like Donna, who had a healthy marriage for over twenty-five years. She was instrumental in helping me walk through those early years of being a wife to David. I also read books to learn healthy marriage and communication skills and discovered I had many negative thought patterns relating to how to behave around men, handed down by toxic role models (i.e., Mom with her many failed and abusive relationships and Grandpa Willie with his angry reign over my childhood home). I had unwittingly carried them right into my marriage.

I started to see areas of unforgiveness I had held in my heart for my mother and grandfather, as well as my other abusers. I learned I wouldn't be able to move forward until I let them go. The idea of remaining "stuck" was a huge motivator to learn how to make this happen. So, I started studying forgiveness and its releasing power. I allowed God to open my past and do His work, and I allowed myself to trust someone enough to talk to fully about my past. I learned how to deal with my emotions and do my best to diffuse arguments, give David space and learn to walk away, and I saw a gradual transformation began to take place. Now, if a confrontation started to arise with David, I could recognize those triggers, take a step back, pray, and calm myself down instead of emotionally losing control.

My personal time of prayer and meditation also was instrumental in dealing with my negative thought patterns. The mind is an immensely powerful tool. Left unchecked, the negative thoughts that play repeatedly in your thoughts can overwhelm you. Learning to take control of them early on was a major key to overcoming the toxic behavior that contributed to the issues early on in my marriage.

In turn, David learned to deal with his anger issues and used more self-control in how he handled situations. God began to heal his heart and mind too. We both pursued personal counseling for help in addressing his past and habitual issues. One successful strategy we implemented was a "time-out moment." When David wanted to have a discussion while he was angry, I would raise my hand and say, "I need us to take a time-out." Then we would walk away while emotions were hot. I would lock myself in the bathroom or sit outside on the patio and meditate, listen to positive music, or just think things through to ensure I was not thinking irrationally about the situation and making things worse. The time-out allowed those emotions to cool down so that when we did come back together, we could have a discussion instead of a screaming match, where nobody wins.

This method is still a powerful tool for us both. Now, we value and respect each other where we are versus trying to change each other's personality. This was a process we aggressively pursued for many years, not months. One day, we'll write our marriage book and tell our transformative marriage story.

Looking back on our journey, I can now see how David was and still is the primary instrument used to shape my character. He has pushed me to stand on my own two feet, to debate or argue my point, and to not cave in to emotional outbursts or crying when things go awry. And I believe I have also had a heavy role in shaping his character. Thought patterns and habits that we both knew and practiced were destructive to our marriage and needed to change in order for us to survive as a unit. We have experienced transformation together, often through trial-by-fire situations. God has used our marriage to each other to expose and chisel away the hardest parts of our hearts, the places where toxic thinking was set in stone, and freed each of us.

David and I have also been one another's greatest change-agent support. Throughout our marriage, we've learned how to work *together* to get through challenges and problems. Communication, understanding, and valuing the other's differences were key to growth and success during those early years and are still so today.

David and I have been married for thirty-one years as of the writing of this book, and we're still going strong!

MY GROWING FAMILY

Through those first two tumultuous years of our marriage, we wanted to keep Crystaline sheltered from all of our woes. Part of our daily routine was to pray with her every night at bedtime. We taught her how to thank God and pray for people and other age-appropriate prayers for a three- to-five-year-old.

Then she started taking it to a different level. One night while we were saying her nighttime prayers, Crystaline asked God for a brother. David and I both looked at each other in shock, wondering, *Wow! What will we do if we don't have a boy?*

Like her Grandma Grace, she didn't back down. She kept praying and praying for that baby brother until one day in January 1993, I discovered I was pregnant. This was a different experience altogether from my first pregnancy at seventeen, because my husband and I had created our first human being together out of the love and passion we shared.

In September 1993, Caleb entered the world. He was over eight pounds and twenty-one and a half inches long with a full head of hair, and he came out like a little man, independent as heck. Because he was such a big baby, I never felt like I had a newborn; he wore clothes the size of a three-month-old baby the day we took him home from the hospital! That kid today is six-foot-five, the tallest members of our entire family. I'm told he gets his height from my dad's Yugoslavian genes and grandfather Willie's Spanish genes.

Pure and simple, God used Caleb to teach us to love. Because David and I had so much baggage from our past and early marriage, we had no clue what real selfless love looked like. We really struggled to demonstrate it to each other and to our daughter Crystaline in the truest sense of the word. We did our best, but we came up short every time. Too much time was wasted getting caught up in arguments over things that really didn't matter in the whole big scheme of things.

But everything changed when Caleb was born. He was the happiest and most carefree baby and toddler you could ever meet. All three of us were utterly in love with him. Crystaline would not leave his side. Caleb was her playmate, and as soon as he could walk, he followed her around like she was his mother. He adored his sister. They were and still are very close, even now as adults. And David was completely committed to his son. I had never seen him more obsessed with anyone. He did everything for that baby boy.

Since we were both working parents, we had to learn how to divide and conquer the family duties after we got home each night around 6:00 p.m. We learned how to be a team in baths, schoolwork, playtime, dinner, cleaning—you name it. David was engaged, front and center. He never missed a baseball game or football practice, supporting and coaching Caleb his whole life. Since David's father had died when he was five and not one member of his family ever went to one of his games or sports activities during his childhood or teen years, he was determined to never allow his children to feel that gaping hole of not having a father or feeling supported.

Then in 1994, we took the next big step in our journey and bought our first home together. It was a huge accomplishment for two people who grew up in environments that did so little, if anything, to encourage or demonstrate owning a home, pursuing a career instead of a job, marrying the love of our lives, and having a two-parent household. It was all a dream come true, and we were thankful to God for His blessing and all the new things we were experiencing in our young family.

We continued to work on our own issues of emotional pain and anger. I also took the principles of patience, kindness, grace, and forgiveness that Donna had helped me with and applied them to our marriage, and David reciprocated. To this day, he admits that I am the one who has mastered de-escalating problems and being the peacemaker in the family, for sure!

Although we made many mistakes, we were committed to taking the good, tossing out the bad, and moving forward.

FORGIVENESS—THE CATALYST FOR CHANGE

While David and I were successful in forgiving each other, my forgiving my mother was quite a bit more challenging. Nevertheless, it had to be done. At about age twenty-five, four years into my marriage, I went to her and asked for her forgiveness. At first, she was surprised, then confused. With a smile and furrowed brow, she asked, "Forgive you for what, Becky?"

"For all of the hate toward you that I've been holding on to all of these years." I searched her eyes for any signs of recognition, of understanding, but found none. She just couldn't understand why I was asking for her forgiveness. It wasn't until later that I realized that she never fully grasped the ways she had hurt us in those early years—she didn't blame herself any more than she blamed us.

But in this moment, for me, her response didn't matter. I was determined not to make this about what she did and didn't do. I pushed through to release her. As a result, I learned that forgiving her wasn't just for her; it was for me as well. It was a huge step in the process of healing my own heart and eradicating all the power she had had over me through my hurt and anger toward her.

Through this process of forgiveness, my relationship with Mom then began to undergo a significant change. For the first time, my heart felt true compassion for her. For the first time, I was able to look beyond her mess or current issues and deep into her soul to realize how very much she loved us. I was able to see how her intentions remained good even when her actions were hurtful and how her struggle with mental illness and addiction had ill-equipped her to deal with her own past, her own trauma.

I also began to see how shame had built a wall around me that kept me from accepting love from or trusting others, including my own husband. As I said, David was my knight in shining armor—in many ways, I looked up to him. Yet when David tried to extend love to me, I recoiled in shame. I never felt like I deserved him. I thought, *If he finds out who I really am, what my past has been, he won't love me anymore.* Once I was finally able to acknowledge the power that shame had over me, I was able to begin healing from it.

When I stopped condemning myself, there was no one left to condemn me—not God, not David, not anyone.

ENTER GOVERNOR GEORGE W. BUSH

My family had come such a long way. Looking back, I can now see that my transformational journey was just picking up speed and was about to venture into territories I never dreamed of.

And I couldn't have done it without my mentor Donna. She held my hand through it all with patience and grace and taught me how to be a career woman. She backed up her belief in me by sending me to trainings and promoting me each year, and with each promotion, my salary grew. Eventually, she decided to send me to supervisor training, a key next step in my career growth.

After a comprehensive combination of training and hands-on learning in 1992, she promoted me as a supervisor of the HR department for the State of Texas. I was happy with my new position, recognizing it as a huge accomplishment for a high school drop-out with a GED who grew up in the hood.

Then Kay Bailey Hutchison ran for U.S. Senate, and Donna left the state treasury. Although I was happy for Donna's new opportunity, I was admittedly fearful for a moment. She had been the one steady woman in my life and my rock at the treasury department. Would I be okay without her? What about when I needed support? Who would I go to?

Donna assured me she would not be far away and that I could always call on her for mentoring or support. That invitation gave me great peace. I then recognized it as an opportunity to spread my wings and get to know other bosses who in turn could help me grow.

When we said our goodbyes, neither of us knew our separation would be short-term. In January 1995, a year later, Dana called me with some wonderful news. Because George W. Bush had just been elected governor of Texas, he had hired her as his state HR director.

My heart filled with joy for her success. Then she took me completely by surprise: "Rebecca, there is no one I would love to have more than you on my team with Governor Bush. Come be my deputy director for HR."

THE OPPORTUNITY TO SERVE

I felt like I was in heaven, literal heaven. The opportunity to work for a governor, work with Donna again, *and* be promoted to deputy director! I felt like I was walking on air. I walked into the treasurer's office and happily resigned.

My new position started me down the path of establishing myself as an HR expert, and Donna was a huge part of that. She pushed me out of my comfort zone and challenged me through special assignments. She wanted me to figure them out on my own and then execute them. Many times when I asked her for help, her response was, "How would you do it? You tell me." After finding the solutions, I could go back and use her as a sounding board. It was true hands-on learning as you go. To this day, there is nothing I won't undertake to learn with boldness.

My position also gave me exposure to senior-manager-level meetings, which was an education in itself and provided opportunities for continued growth. I learned quickly that Governor Bush always surrounded himself with exceptionally smart people, professionals with acclaimed experience and multiple degrees—all of which I didn't have. I observed, learned from, and tried to emulate them. I was a sponge soaking it all up! As a fly on the wall at important meetings, watching how people communicated in a roundtable setting, or taking the lead in various initiatives so that I could learn alongside them, I was determined to expand my experience and mindset. I figured if I could learn from them, get close to their inner circle, perhaps I could advance myself to the next level. This new role started my passion to serve people in the HR business.

REWARDS OF STAYING TEACHABLE

David was also progressing in his career in the tech industry. He's incredibly smart, in part because he's always reading, feeding his insatiable appetite for lifelong learning. It's not uncommon to see him going back and forth, reading two books at the same time. When I first married him, I often caught him reading the dictionary. When I asked him why, he responded, "I'm expanding my vocabulary."

I wasn't as strong in this area and struggled with reading comprehension. David knew its power both personally and professionally and encouraged me to work on my reading skills. Up for the challenge, I immersed myself in books to absorb all I could about leadership, management, communication, and self-help from renowned authors who knew a thing or two about success. My human resource training was ongoing, and the constant reading of HR policies, practices, and case studies was essential to my success and path forward, even more so since I didn't have a formal degree.

My efforts paid off as new high-level opportunities presented themselves. After being in my job for a couple of years, Donna wanted to propel my training and development into senior management. She nominated me to be part of a select group of Texas state government senior managers slated to attend the prestigious Governor's Executive Development Program at the LBJ School of Public Affairs.

Governor Bush signed off on my candidacy. His nomination made me feel honored and incredibly humbled. Not only did it afford me the opportunity to expand my network statewide, but it also gave me direct hands-on learning in senior leadership.

Upon completing that program and receiving my certification, I felt more confident than ever to serve in a senior managerial role.

CLIMBING THE LADDER WITH BUSH

In 1997, Governor Bush ran for his second term, although there were rumors that he might run for president in 2000. Donna resigned from her role as HR director to lead another office within the governor's administration. Before she left, she announced to me in private, "Rebecca, I'm going to recommend you to the chief of staff to take my place as HR director."

Initially, I was terrified and froze! Pulling myself together, I replied, "Wait a minute, Donna. I'm nowhere near ready. Who's going to help me? You've been with me so long, how do you know I can do your job?"

Her eyes twinkled as a big grin spread across her face. "Rebecca, you are an eagle, and it's time for you to fly out of the nest and soar on your own, outside of my shadow."

She was right because soar I did! It's amazing what happens when someone believes in you. I had potential, but because I was so insecure, I didn't feel like I was ready. Someone had to push me out of the nest for me to fly.

In 1997, Governor Bush was reelected with 70 percent of the vote, and I began my journey into senior management as I stepped into my mentor's shoes and assumed the role of HR director. Only highly educated, credentialed people were normally selected for these positions, so I knew my selection was due to favor, hard work, and gaining the trust of senior leaders. I tried hard to not squander that favor and disappoint the belief others had in me. Never once did I let on (at least not in public) that I was intimidated or unqualified for the role. Under Donna's leadership, I had learned to demonstrate self-assurance.

EQUIPPING AND PREPARING

David has always been a confident man, so when I felt weak or unqualified, I went to him and him only because I had learned over the years to never show these feelings of inadequacy to others. David always gave me a pep talk. We would talk through the issue or circumstance, and I gained confidence in the role over time.

Early on in my career as a senior manager, I was confronted by another top senior leader known for being a bit of a bully in his management style. He was my superior, and I was called to speak to him about a decision I had made that he didn't agree with.

When I walked into his Texas Capitol office, he rose from his chair. His stern expression told me he was probably going to chew me out. "Have a seat," he stated, motioning for me to sit down.

Seeing his grand desk positioned higher than the chair he offered, I replied, "No thank you. I'll stand." I didn't want to give him the satisfaction of towering over me in an effort to intimidate me.

He continued standing as well.

After his ten-minute rant, I quickly stated, "If you're done, I'd like to help clarify why I made that decision. Even if you feel it was wrong, I am the HR director, and the governor pays me to make personnel decisions. If I make one in error, I'll own it, but I prefer to talk through the rationale behind my decision so that you can gain a bit more understanding." I explained my reasons, standing eye to eye with him. He was a very tall man, about six-foot three, but with my heels on, I stood close to his height.

After my explanation, he sat down. "I'll talk with you later," he stated and dismissed me.

I left his office, rushed immediately to the bathroom, and cried my eyes out. Then I called David and told him about the incident. I needed his counsel.

He didn't let me down. "Be confident in your stance but respectful," he encouraged. "Don't let him bother you. Let that whole incident roll off your back and move forward."

It was the first time I'd had an intense encounter with a man who was in leadership over me. I wasn't about to let him see me weak. A few days later, he called to apologize for his tone. From then on, he treated me with a bit more respect in the role.

Following David's advice, I continued to move forward in my new position. My new boss was a woman named Vickers, a no-nonsense senior leader. She oversaw all management functions including HR, IT, procurement, Office of Finance, the mail room, and other miscellaneous offices. She had seen me in action working for Donna, but I had little direct access to her until we began interacting in my new role.

Vickers and I got along great. We were a well-oiled management team. She had just as much confidence in me as Donna did but without the "mother hen" personality and intimacy—our relationship was strictly professional. Her demeanor actually helped encourage my independence and growth into senior leadership. She was my superior, but she embraced my role and afforded me the opportunity to govern in it. And I was ready. It was the next level of growth I needed to prepare me for one of the biggest steps I would soon be taking in my career.

Vickers reported to Clay, the governor's chief of staff. Clay was a Yale-MIT graduate, about six-foot-three, and very direct and no-nonsense in his style as well. Governor Bush surrounded himself with people like this. Perhaps that's why I now have that same management style—what you see is what you get with me.

Vickers gave me full access to communicate directly with Clay, who was quite interested in HR and people. Under his leadership, I began to see the action behind the scenes in the Texas Capitol. He would come to me directly for all HR-related issues and then operate in a hands-on way, bypassing the hierarchy usually found in government.

My three years as HR director stretched me tremendously, not only in my career but also in my home life as a wife and mom. David had also continued to accelerate in his high-tech career at Sematech, a manufacturing company in Austin. For me, it was about wearing many hats—mom, wife, director, confidant, home financial manager, cook, errand runner, and all-around one-stop shop for all things family and career—and figuring out how to navigate it all well. Inevitably, some balls dropped, and tension was high at times in our young home. I had to learn everything from the ground up by listening to positive messages, reading, being mentored, and watching others succeed. I was determined to get it right.

THE PRESSURE INTENSIFIES

The behind-the-scenes George W. Bush was a man of integrity and warmth, which carried over into his leadership style. Because I was in charge of hiring his staff, he took a special interest in knowing me and paid several visits to my office. It was not uncommon for him to pop in out of the blue. I knew when he was in the office because I'd hear that good ole Texas drawl from the hallway asking, "Becca, how are you, hon'?" Bush was famous for assigning nicknames to his senior-level management.

He always cared deeply about the people who worked for him, whether they were staff or interns. I was fortunate to experience firsthand the way he valued people. His listening skills and ability to remember anyone's name after hearing it once made people feel special. As I grew in my career and expanded my knowledge, I always tried to follow suit with this trait of knowing and loving people.

Governor Bush also loved his constituents. Oftentimes, his director of correspondence would get a letter in the mail that tugged at the heartstrings, and he ensured that it was personally delivered to the governor so he could read it. One story stands out distinctly. Governor Bush was a runner. Every day, he would run at Town Lake in downtown Austin. Every so often, he would run on public trails, followed closely by Texas security detail on bikes.

A young man about sixteen years old wrote a letter to the governor, telling him about a bad accident where he'd been thrown from his bicycle. He had been a runner for his school's track team, but the accident paralyzed him from the waist down. He was working hard, doing therapy every day to walk. He asked the governor, "If I learn to walk again, can we run together?"

Governor Bush told him in a personal handwritten note, "You focus on walking again, and yes, we will run together soon." And run they did. A year after that young man's accident, he joined the governor on Town Lake for that run (or more like power walk).

Governor Bush also wanted to meet his interns personally every semester, which made an impression on me. Part of my job was to staff the statewide governor's internship program for both the fall and summer semesters. He asked me to organize a lunch in the mansion for the new intern class.

One of my proudest hires from the internship program was a young man named Jodey out of Texas Tech. After his internship, we hired him to work full time for the governor. He then went on to work for President Bush in DC and is now a U.S. Congressman. I'm so proud of Jodey and all he has accomplished.

During that particular intern session, I sat around a table with fifteen interns as they asked the governor very intimate questions about his office, such as the decision-making process he undertook daily on critical issues. Then one of the students boldly asked, "Are you thinking seriously about running for president? What's a major factor that would make you consider doing so?"

The governor's answer taught me how deeply he was committed to his family. "Well, Jenna and Barbara, my girls, don't want me to do it, so they'd have to come around." Another top consideration was whether he could take the people he most trusted with him to Washington DC. He would not go it alone without them. "Next to my family and girls," he said, "that would be top of the list to consider running."

He then added that in the meantime, he would be focusing on the task at hand—governing the great State of Texas. He then gave a talk on having the right people around you to counsel you, support you, and help you govern.

AN INVITATION TO SERVE THE PRESIDENT OF THE UNITED STATES (POTUS)

Those six years serving under Governor Bush and working with Donna, Vickers, and Clay shaped not only my style of management and love for people but also my spine—the resolve to stand firm for what I believe and not allow anything, no matter what, to shake my foundation.

The last few months before the 2000 presidential election, Governor Bush asked Clay to gauge the interest of staff who might want to be considered for a move to DC should he be elected. This is part of the process when an elected official runs for higher office. It was important to make sure those who knew him or worked for him were included for consideration, particularly those key to advancing his Texas policies.

One day, we were in Clay's office at the Texas Capitol, discussing this process since my role was the HR director. We went down the list of people with a high potential to serve. It was really important to Clay that the governor's staff of 280 employees felt included, or at least considered, in the process.

As I sat there in front of Clay's desk taking notes, he looked up at me and said, "Governor Bush asked me today, 'Do you think Rebecca would be interested in going to DC if I were elected?' Of course, I told him, 'Oh no, I don't think so. She and David just built a house, and David just got a new job. I doubt she'll want to go.'"

I almost fell out of my seat, shocked that my name would come up as part of that impressive list. "Clay," I responded, "of course I would want to at least talk about it. Why did you tell him I wasn't interested?" I paused for a moment, trying to process this news while Clay studied me. Then I added, "Me? Wow! That's amazing! Why would Governor Bush ask about me? I don't know anything about DC or serving in a presidential administration. Would it really be an opportunity for me to consider?" I was blown away.

He nodded. "Rebecca, he very much knows who you are and about your work. I'll go back and tell him you're interested. Should he be elected, we'll discuss at that time where there might be a fit for you."

I went home still stunned and shared the news with David. I asked, "David, do you think we should consider it?" We hadn't even thought about it, because never in a million years did I believe it was even a possibility. I hadn't worked on a campaign; I was in a civilian state job with tenure; we had just built our new dream home a year before; the kids were in a great new school; and David was just a few months into his newly promoted job at Applied Materials. Everything seemed perfect.

But after that conversation with Clay, David and I began to really contemplate, pray, and seek counsel from those closest to us about whether we should throw my name in the hat for consideration.

LEAVING FOR DC

The election in November 2000 was highly contested due to a recount in Florida, and our lives hung in the balance for the next five weeks. The courts could rule one direction or another soon, so I had to continue forward with the potential transition of the new governor, Rick Perry. At the time, he had been serving as lieutenant governor of Texas.

At the same time, part of my job as the human resources director was to collect resumés and prepare packets from the existing gubernatorial staff who wanted to be considered in the possible transition to DC. All of it involved HR at the state level. But the thought of going to DC myself would not leave my mind. Clay's words of the now-president-elect asking about me rang over and over in my head. I lived, slept, and breathed the possibility and what it would mean for us as a family overall.

Finally, after weeks of recounts across numerous counties in Florida, the election was called, and Governor Bush became the official president-elect. Shortly afterward Vickers, Clay, and others on the governor's senior team left for DC along with key people from Bush's presidential campaign. It was time to set up the official transition office in DC. I was asked to stay behind and transition in the new governor. At that point, there was no discussion about what role in DC I might take.

I had been a "good soldier," but when I was left behind for that time, my heart sank. I started to doubt my potential to join the transition team in DC. Many negative thoughts came in where I questioned if I was a fit or a priority. It didn't take long for me to get rid of them as I focused on fulfilling my duties for the State of Texas.

On a Sunday nearing the last day in December, I received an email from Clay. He had not forgotten about me. He had one position left on his presidential personnel transition team, and he wanted me to join him in DC.

His deputy called the next morning and explained that I would initially support a small team, but after Bush took the oath of office, I would be placed in the White House Presidential Personnel Office (or PPO), working for POTUS and Clay as one of five directors managing the hiring process for the president's 4,000 federal appointments.

I couldn't believe my ears! The job was so much bigger than the job I had in Texas, bigger than I ever expected. I would oversee 1,200 positions for the president of the United States, a mind-blowing opportunity!

By then, David and I felt good about the decision to move. I packed my bags and was off to DC within five days. The recount had put us behind in schedule, so there was no time to waste.

David and I agreed that he would stay behind with the kids and put the house on the market. He would come up for the inauguration and stay afterwards to find us a house. DC is a very expensive place to live and doesn't really cater to families, so we wanted to find an area with good schools, safe communities, and more landscape and home for our buck. We had heard that living in an area close to the train or metro was essential due to the tremendous traffic in the DC area. Many commuters used the rail system to commute into the district.

Fortunately, we didn't have to look for long. We found a beautiful Victorian-style house nestled in a cul-de-sac in Manassas, Virginia, less than a mile from the VRE (Virginia Railway Express) train and about twenty minutes from a metro stop.

Also, while David was in DC, I had access to amazing VIP post-inauguration events for President Bush. Neither David nor I had ever been to a presidential inauguration, so this was a first for us! The incredible festivities lasted a week—parties, ceremonies, events, and presidential balls. I felt like Cinderella all over again. Never did we dream we'd be given such a life-altering experience.

Afterwards, David went back to Austin to resign from his job, pull the kids out of school, and get our stuff moved. However, the house didn't sell quickly. So, in early March, David packed up the moving truck anyway and got to DC as quickly as he could. By that time, I hadn't seen him since the inauguration, and I hadn't seen our kids for about eight weeks. I really missed them.

It was wonderful to have us all together again, embarking on this exciting new journey that would provide us with once-in-a-lifetime opportunities we could have never before fathomed.

Little did we know this move would change the trajectory of our lives and careers forever!

Mom Grace drug days 60s

Mom Grace exotic dancer days 60s

Rebecca Lost Girl cover - Age 16

Rebecca pregnant on welfare - Age 18

Supervised visit with Crystaline 1988

Rebecca & David hangout after gang outreach play 1989

Rebecca & David wedding April 1990

Rebecca & David wedding with mom Grace & mom Janie

Rebecca & David wedding with Crystaline

First young family birthday party for Crystaline (cousin Elicia on right)

Rebecca with Crystaline & Caleb 1993

Rebecca & kids 1995—fun day at the park

Texas Governor Bush - Rebecca HR Director 1997

Rebecca with Kay Bailey Hutchison - State Treasury 1993

Contreras family - Governor Bush staff Christmas party 1998

Governor Bush & Donna (Rebecca's "all in mentor" in red) 1997

Rebecca's visit to grandma Keta Marfa Texas 1999

Rebecca & grandma Keta's visit to Austin 2000

Rebecca & Caleb's great grandma Keta 2006

Presidential Inauguration first term Bush 2001

Rebecca & David private invite White House dinner 2001

Presidential personnel - Clay's White House PPO team in Oval 2001

Rebecca's commissioning ceremony in Oval 2001

White House PPO team meeting in Oval (Rebecca in red suit) 2001

Rebecca & boss Clay – critical conversations in Oval 2002

White House staff Christmas party 2002

OAS VIP event - POTUS asks David what he is doing in DC for a job March 2001

WH lawn Marine One landing - David shares with POTUS he is working for him now April 2001

West Wing Rose Garde stroll 2003

Rebecca & David at White House event with Clay, boss and mentor 2003

Crystaline & Caleb settled in VA

First family visit to VA Blue Ridge Mountains

Rebecca & her WH PPO team, VIP tour Holocaust Museum, a POTUS Board

Rebecca's kids attend WH staff Easter Egg Roll

Kids join mom on WH lawn Easter Egg Roll

Contreras family night at the Kennedy Center – VIP POTUS box

Rebecca & David invite VIP Arts Event

Movie premier VIP badge

Rebecca & David movie premier "Sum of All Fears" VIP event

Rebecca & David meet Morgan Freeman

Rebecca Red Carpet - Meets Ben Affleck

Rebecca & David meet Esai Morales at VIP Gala

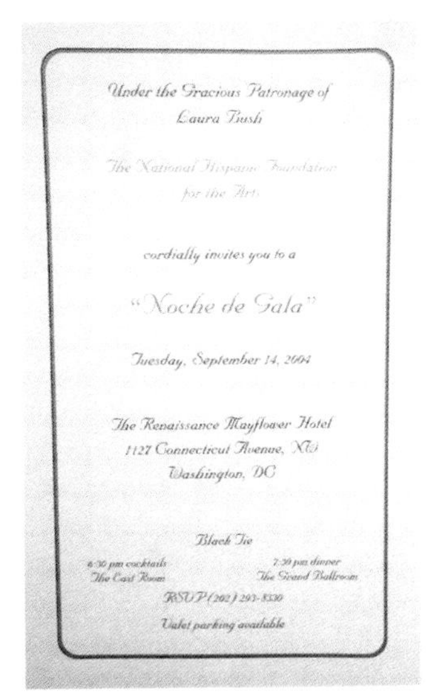

Under the Gracious Patronage of
Laura Bush

The National Hispanic Foundation
for the Arts

cordially invites you to a

"Noche de Gala"

Tuesday, September 14, 2004

The Renaissance Mayflower Hotel
1127 Connecticut Avenue, NW
Washington, DC

Black Tie

6:30 pm cocktails
The East Room

7:30 pm dinner
The Grand Ballroom

RSVP (202) 293-8330

Valet parking available

Ms. Bush invite to VIP arts event

Rebecca's WH PPO Boards & Commission team 2001 (with boss Clay)

Rebecca meets Nicholas Cage Red Carpet movie event

Rebecca & Oscar de la Renta VIP Luncheon 2002

Rebecca addresses Grand Ole Opry group

Rebecca meets Natalie Cole – Nashville 2005

Grand Ole Opry VIP event with Amy Grant & Vince Gill

POTUS jokes with Rebecca in Oval, telling her she can't leave the White House 2003

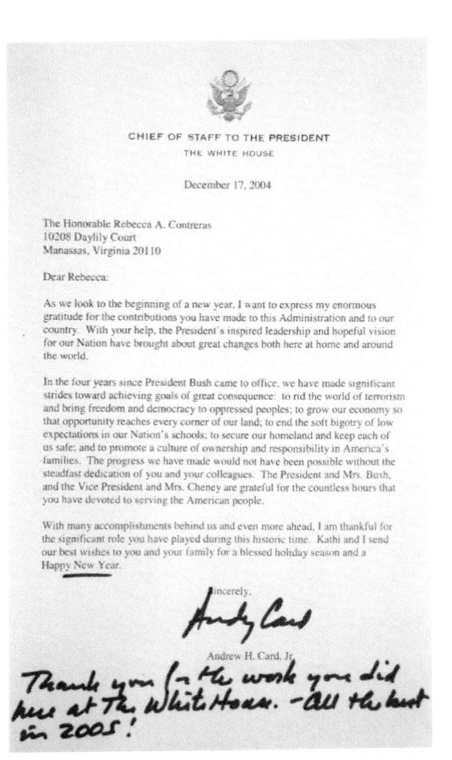

CHIEF OF STAFF TO THE PRESIDENT

THE WHITE HOUSE

December 17, 2004

The Honorable Rebecca A. Contreras
10208 Daylily Court
Manassas, Virginia 20110

Dear Rebecca:

As we look to the beginning of a new year, I want to express my enormous gratitude for the contributions you have made to this Administration and to our country. With your help, the President's inspired leadership and hopeful vision for our Nation have brought about great changes both here at home and around the world.

In the four years since President Bush came to office, we have made significant strides toward achieving goals of great consequence: to rid the world of terrorism and bring freedom and democracy to oppressed peoples; to grow our economy so that opportunity reaches every corner of our land; to end the soft bigotry of low expectations in our Nation's schools; to secure our homeland and keep each of us safe; and to promote a culture of ownership and responsibility in America's families. The progress we have made would not have been possible without the steadfast dedication of you and your colleagues. The President and Mrs. Bush, and the Vice President and Mrs. Cheney are grateful for the countless hours that you have devoted to serving the American people.

With many accomplishments behind us and even more ahead, I am thankful for the significant role you have played during this historic time. Kathi and I send our best wishes to you and your family for a blessed holiday season and a Happy New Year.

Sincerely,

Andy Card

Andrew H. Card, Jr.

Thank you for the work you did here at The White House. - All the best in 2005!

WH Chief of Staff Andy Card post 911 "thank you for serving"

Rebecca hard at work - Presidential Personnel Office 2003

Rebecca's service on the West Point Board NYC 2006

Rebecca having lunch during a board break with West Point cadets 2007

Mom & Caleb during West Point board visit 2007

Contreras family White House lawn 4th of July

POTUS lets Caleb sit in his Oval Office chair 2003

Rebecca's big promotion move to Chief of HR US Treasury with Sec John Snow 2003

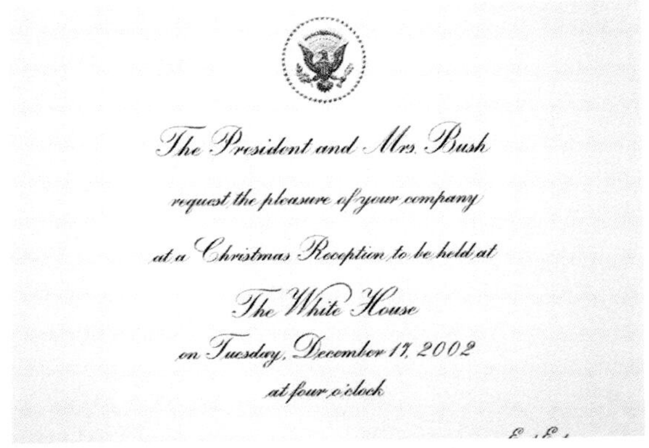
The President and Mrs. Bush
request the pleasure of your company
at a Christmas Reception to be held at
The White House
on Tuesday, December 17, 2002
at four o'clock

Rebecca & David attend White House staff party

White House staff Christmas party with POTUS & FLOTUS

Rebecca & POTUS in Oval Office

Contreras resignation to return to Texas – POTUS personal thank in Oval Office Dec 2004

David & Rebecca Texas Bush Library VIP opening event 2013

Contreras family vacation summer 2018

Mom Grace with her kids (Rebecca's siblings) before depression illness hits hard 2007

David & Rebecca's nonprofit LaunchPad community outreach 2013

CHAPTER FIVE

WASHINGTON DC, A PLANET OF iTS OWN

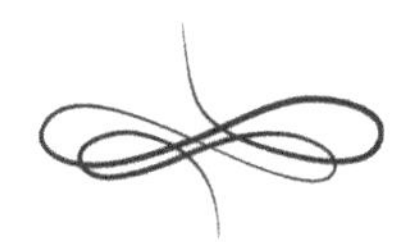

"I am a firm believer in the people. If given the truth, they can be depended upon to meet any national crisis. The great point is to bring them the real facts."

—ABRAHAM LINCOLN

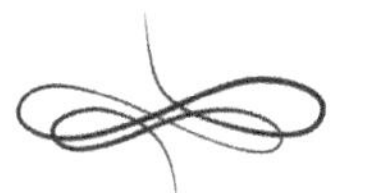

My new job working for a president in DC came with enormous shoes to fill. In the beginning months, I worked seven days a week, fourteen-hour days. The seven of us leading the Presidential Personnel Process already had our hands full with over 4,000 positions to fill in Bush's first term. Add the late start due to the Florida recount, and we were eating, sleeping, and breathing our jobs.

My portfolio was over 1,200 positions strong, and I was in charge of staffing the part-time volunteer presidential boards and commissions. The most powerful undertaking for a president is to make appointments—selecting people from all over the country to serve in important roles. I was told that out of the six commissioned officers managing the appointments process for POTUS, I had the most-coveted portfolio. It allowed me to meet and interview the best and brightest minds who had success in their careers and didn't necessarily need or want to move to DC to take a full-time job. However, they would consider representing POTUS as volunteers on various boards and commissions—boards like the Kennedy Center, West Point Military Academy, Fannie Mae and Freddie Mac, the Holocaust Museum, the President's Council on Physical Fitness, and more than 260 other boards. I also got to hire a talented team of three deputies and one assistant, along with a handful of interns who would come and go every fall during the White House internship program.

Serving in the role of special assistant to the president and associate director of presidential personnel came with its perks. I was told that my commissioned officer status came with the rank of a two-star general as long as I was in the job. I wasn't quite sure what that meant, nor did I care; I was just honored to be serving President Bush. Later, I found out from the experts and those who had been in the job for other presidents that these ranks and titles mattered in DC, especially when it came to people taking you seriously. One of the first things I did was seek out and meet with two former directors who had handled my portfolio for President Bush 41, the president's father. They passed down incredible insights that provided guidance and context for what I was undertaking.

When all staffed up, we started our hard work, which included learning the entire portfolio. I was handed the highly desired black books—three large spiral binders containing Articles of Description for each board and commission in the federal government. Everything we needed to know to complete the portfolio was in them. None of it was automated, and the black books with thousands of pieces of paper were handed down to the incoming staff from administration to administration as a tradition.

My team and I sat on the floor of the Old Executive Office Building until late in the night with those articles spread out in front of us, trying to figure out what was what. Thankfully, I had hired people who were highly educated and much smarter than I was, something I always took pride in doing. Slowly but surely, we made headway. The more we unraveled the process, the closer we got to the solutions.

TOUGH TRANSITIONS

It didn't take long to discover just how much Washington DC was an entirely different planet where some of the brightest and most accomplished people worked and lived. It is known for being a town of haves and have-nots. The haves are educated, know important people, live in fancy row houses, drive fancy cars, hang out in fancy restaurants, and drink fancy wine. Every night, there's a happy hour, important event, or party happening. Being a part of that socialite life is an important piece to the puzzle of true success in DC.

For me, it was never about belonging to that clique; I was there to serve the president. But working in the White House magnified my insecurities. I lacked both education and an understanding of DC politics. Many times, I felt out of my element, inadequate, and outright unqualified for the role. Additionally, I was overwhelmed as a wife and mom with a young family who had just moved our entire world 1,500 miles across the country to live in a state we didn't know in a location where not one family member or close confidant was with us.

During our entire marriage, we had been surrounded by family, and at that time, David's family was very close. Every weekend in Austin, we ate Sunday dinner at his mom's (a.k.a. Grandma Jaine), and we actively engaged in hangouts or camping trips with his brothers, sister, and cousins. My mom also lived there, and we had a strong support system in our church community at Shoreline with many close couples we called friends.

My husband had walked away from a ten-year career in the tech industry so that we could move to DC to serve POTUS. He had no job, and we had gone from two incomes down to one income in a place where the cost of living was 25 to 30 percent higher. We closed on our new home in early March and had two mortgages coming due in sixty days. The home in Austin was still sitting empty, so we decided to lease it out with an agent working around the clock to find a tenant for us.

I was in over my head with the stress and pressure of my all-consuming White House job. My long hours left David to bear the brunt of our transition by himself, assimilating us into our home, community, and schools, and taking on the role of father, mother, chef, and homework helper. Up until I left for DC in early January, David had never cooked a meal or handled many of the domestic tasks. He was always the professional dish washer, and he helped with housecleaning and homework, but he'd never handled tasks such as doctor appointments, laundry, grocery shopping, handling the finances, or cooking. He stepped up to the plate like a champ.

As a result of my long hours at work, Crystaline and David were it for each other. Crystaline was in middle school and in one of the toughest times in her young life as a preteen girl. She has always been expressive and passionate, as is David. They are both very much alike in that they oftentimes try to convince each other of their opinion while they argue their case, no matter what the topic. They were like oil and water back then, and I wasn't around much to act as a buffer between them.

David alone had to contend with Crystaline kicking and screaming before, during, and after our move to DC. She did not want to be there and didn't understand why she had to leave all her family and friends in the middle of eighth grade and move to a place where she didn't know a soul. Then she would have to start high school as a freshman in a new school again full of strangers. This whole environment lent itself to turmoil, especially with a resistant eighth-grade girl. David struggled early on to deal with the drama of this transition for his young daughter and would often call me to "talk some sense into her." In the end, we made it work. Within a week of arriving in Virginia, he had both of the kids settled into their new schools in Manassas.

We also found out we had great neighbors. About a month after moving in, I finally made it around to meet them, going door to door on a Saturday. They were all stay-at-home moms who all happened to be fans of President Bush. It was a wonderful experience getting to know them. One of them said, "We were beginning to think this Rebecca didn't really exist!" and they laughed it off.

These wonderful neighbors became a great support system for us during the four years we were in the area. They generously opened up their homes to our children. Little did we know, less than nine months later our family would be rocked by 9/11, and we would need them more than ever.

A HAUNTING FROM MY PAST

The past has a way of coming back to bite you. I've lived with regrets from mine, even though I thought it was behind me, especially after working for Governor Bush for six years. Not so. It had only been lying dormant, waiting to emerge when it had the potential to do the most damage. Once I moved to Washington DC, my past ran after me fast and furiously. Within the first few months in my new role, it caught up to me.

On that crisp morning in early March, I had just arrived at my office in the Eisenhower Executive Office Building, also called the Old Executive Office Building. I put my purse in my desk drawer when someone knocked on my door. Before I could respond, two men in suits walked in. "Mrs. Contreras," they said, flipping open their badge holders, "we're the Secret Service team in charge of handling your security clearance for your role in the White House. We need to talk to you. Do you have a few minutes?"

Immediately, my heart sank while my pulse raced. All kinds of questions flooded my mind—*What do they want? Are they looking for something? Have they found something?*

The only thing lingering was the twenty-five-page security clearance application I had submitted about sixty days earlier. I had been given interim clearance based on my clean record until my background investigation was cleared. And it had yet to be cleared. When serving a president that process can take anywhere from six to twelve weeks, sometimes longer depending on the individual's background.

The application asked just about everything—the applicant's background, family, and friends, both present and past. I was forthright with my answers, disclosing my drug use and the mischief I had engaged in during my teen years.

I used the overview description to share my stories of being a single mom and my rough childhood. I didn't have an arrest record, even though I had put myself in precarious situations as a teenager. Fortunately, I always managed to weasel my way out of them. So, I thanked God for protecting me from harm and a life of crime.

I calmed myself down and forced a smile. "Of course," I responded and waved my hand toward the two chairs in front of my desk, "have a seat."

They did and then pulled out a thick file that looked like it had hundreds of pages in it. "Mrs. Contreras, this is your file. We've been conducting our investigation of you for two months to determine your suitability for a security clearance to serve the president. We've discovered some disturbing alleged behaviors and other matters, and we'd like to ask you about them. We will remind you that any embellishment of the truth or lack of telling the truth, and you can be prosecuted for a felony to the fullest extent of the law."

I gulped. "Yes sir, I understand. Please ask away."

They went back to my teen years and unveiled incidents and behaviors, mostly around my use of drugs and party lifestyle. With no emotion they asked, "Are these true?"

"Yes," I answered, trying to make my voice sound strong when I felt anything but.

They divulged their notes on my past friends and asked me if I had relations with particular people. It seemed like I answered their questions for hours. Every single answer I gave was with thoughtfulness and truth. I attempted to frame them with "I did that because my home situation was X or Y. I didn't have any direction or discipline in my life and was quite troubled in my teen years."

They took notes the entire time. A frown appeared on one man's face, revealing his displeasure with my answers. I wanted to ask them, "Didn't you ever do anything stupid when you were seventeen or eighteen that you regret today?" But I didn't. I figured my posture and position needed to remain courteous, humble, and contrite over my bad decisions.

Then they got around to asking about Juan. "Mrs. Contreras, we understand you were involved with a drug dealer with a long criminal record by the name of Juan X. We also understand that he's the father of your daughter Crystaline. Is that true?"

At that point, I nearly broke down and cried. It took everything within me to stay calm and quiet my spirit while my heart raced faster. I took a deep breath and let it out. "Yes sir, it's true."

"How did you meet Juan?" he asked. "Please explain the full context of your relationship with him. And I'll remind you, Mrs. Contreras, we have all the records from the interviews with people in your past, so you should think twice before you decide to steer away from the truth."

I went on for about thirty minutes, giving them an overview of how I met and got involved with Juan and my relationship of nearly three years with him just prior to his arrest by the FBI. I explained that I was only sixteen when I met him, and he was much older than me. It wasn't until I was deep into the relationship under his abusive grip that I realized he was a criminal and a drug dealer. I added, "I was never involved in his criminal activity or business." (Yet *another* God-saved moment). I explained how abusive he was and described how he almost killed me and how he threatened to cut up my face if I ever left him.

They asked questions about their reports and the allegations they had heard about Juan. I was able to confirm them through my stories of interactions with him and with what I had witnessed and heard. Their eyebrows furrowed and jaw muscles tightened the more I collaborated their suspicions of Juan and his activities.

I ended by saying, "Please consider, if I were lying and involved in his crimes, don't you think the FBI would have interrogated me or found out about my involvement when they prosecuted him? I was never called, never approached, never searched. So please believe me when I tell you I had zero involvement with his lifestyle or crime. The biggest mistake of my young teen life was to get involved with him. Again, I was sixteen. He has no involvement in my life now; my husband made sure of that. David is the father to my daughter, and Juan is not on her birth certificate, so he's a forgotten memory of my past. We don't expect him ever to surface again."

They asked a few other questions about some incidents that simply didn't happen, not even close. I swore they were not true. "I have no idea why someone in my past would say those things about me. They're lies," I insisted.

One of the agents stated, "Mrs. Contreras, with Juan hanging over your past, what confidence can we have that he won't come back into your life and demand attention? Juan is a criminal. What confidence do you have that if you're given a security clearance, you won't jeopardize the president or highly classified information just to save yourself or your daughter?"

That was when I broke. I could feel the tears well up in my eyes, but I didn't care anymore. "With all due respect, I have survived this man and am where I am today because I am resilient and a survivor. I have a good husband who protects me, a family, and a reputable career now. I am *not* the person I used to be. Please trust me when I tell you I am not the old Rebecca those pages in your files describe. Please don't hold my past over me and keep me from my purpose. I love President Bush; he's been good to me and my family, and I am forever in debt to him for giving me this once-in-a-lifetime opportunity. I would *never,* and I mean *never* do anything to jeopardize or hurt this president. Period. I stand by my character, my change, and my record of being trustworthy and plead with you to consider the last thirteen years of my record and life and not just four of my wayward teen years. I own up to the mistakes of my past, but they don't define who I am today."

The other agent shrugged. "Well, we don't determine final suitability; the White House Counsel does. We'll wrap up our case and make our recommendation to the Counsel." They stood up and left.

I watched as they walked down the hallway and then closed and locked my door so no one would come in. I made my way back to my chair, fell into it, and allowed myself to cry for probably ten minutes or so. I cried harder than I have ever cried before. I felt devastated, depleted, exhausted, and overwhelmingly fearful. Voices in my head reminded me, "See, the real you is coming out. You're a loser. You won't survive this. You're a failure, and now everyone you have worked with for over six years will know who you really are."

I was falling apart emotionally and felt like I couldn't breathe. Then a thought popped into my head: *I have to call David. He has to know what just happened. He'll know what to do.*

My voice quivered as I told him about the incident. David, in his usual in-command form, responded, "Babe, here's what we're going to do. First, I'm going to pray for you so that those feelings of fear and doubt won't overwhelm you anymore. You need to walk in peace and calm yourself down. Second, call Clay right now and tell him you must see him immediately for an urgent meeting. Then walk over to his office in the West Wing and tell him *all* about your past. Tell him what just happened, and tell him your commitment to serve. Clay will know what to do, but your past record must come to him from *you, not* the Secret Service. *You* must disclose your past to him before they make their recommendation to Counsel."

I was so ashamed, and the last thing I wanted to do was share the awful incidents of my past to the one person I admired the most, but I knew it had to be done.

We then prayed together, and miraculously, talking through it with David and centering my emotions did calm me down. Having David's strength and courage has always been a calming force for me in life. Before we hung up, he reminded me, "Understand that God did not bring us this far to have us fail. God opened the door for this job. You've worked hard for it and have rebuilt your reputation. Stand in confidence, not in fear. You're *not* the same person you were thirteen years ago. You're different and transformed, so believe that, stand on that, and let's agree together that this will not harm you or our family. We will get through this. Also, remember that Clay and the president have confidence in you, or they would not have asked you to join the team. Stand on that. You can overcome this hiccup."

I called Clay. Fortunately, his schedule happened to be open, and he was able to meet with me right away. My frame of mind going into that meeting was critical to my overall success. I needed to collect my thoughts, calm my emotions, and map out a plan on next steps.

Clay is an extraordinary leader and mentor. I have never met anyone like him. During the entire time I've known him, now over twenty years, he has always made time for me and answered my calls and emails, usually within minutes of sending them. At that time, he was the busiest person on the planet, overseeing the presidential transition team with those aforementioned 4,000 personnel appointments as well as the process for high-ranking presidential positions, head cabinet members, congressional members, top White House staff, you name it, all of whom called on him 24/7. But he has always made time for me.

Now I follow suit in my own leadership style. I'm never too busy to listen to my staff's issues or concerns. Together we solve problems, no matter how difficult or challenging they are. I am here. This is how I have led my team and how I now lead my company. I believe that the overall skills of listening and acting to solve a problem are top qualities every leader must possess.

COVERED IN MERCY

Clay's office was a two- to three-minute walk inside the White House complex from the Executive Office of the President. As I entered the West Wing, I decided to take the longer and more scenic route through the lawn past the press corps cameras.

My access badge was navy blue, which meant I had full access to walk the grounds, the West Wing, and the White House—one of the perks of a commissioned officer on staff. I paced slowly, prayed, took deep breaths, and declared to myself in a whisper, "All will be well. I have confidence that God is with me, and I will overcome. I will not fear or doubt. We've got this." My pacing turned into a meditation walk to center myself. I thanked God for the air, the beautiful grounds, the opportunity to serve, my family, and everything else that came to mind. It's amazing how refocusing our minds and hearts around positive things and gratitude, instead of fear and negativity, can give us the ability to press forward.

By the time I arrived at the entrance of the West Wing, a tremendous calm overcame my soul. Deep inside I knew, no matter the outcome, it would be okay.

I sat down next to Clay's desk and told him about the incident that had occurred just forty-five minutes earlier, laying out all the details. As I talked, his brow started to furrow, and his face became tense. So, I expanded on my childhood upbringing and past to paint the picture of the environment I grew up in. "Clay," I said, "I'm not making excuses for the mistakes of my past, but I'm not the same woman the Secret Service agents described."

Clay still appeared worried, so I continued to plead my case. I realized that what had just happened could get me fired, ruin my career, and prevent me from going forward. Besides praying, the only action I could take at this point was to fall on Clay's understanding, compassion, and mercy. I then shared with him my transformation story, how I met David, and how, for the first time in my life, I was now part of a loving family.

His demeanor changed. His inner eyebrows went from pointing downward in concern to pointing upward in compassion. I paused, and before I had a chance to speak again, he said, "My goodness, if anyone would have asked me to tell them about Rebecca, I would have said, 'She's the epitome of Hispanic royalty.' How in the world did you survive and overcome such a tumultuous childhood and teen life?"

I told him what had led to my transformation and the details of my turnaround. I added, "I love President Bush and would never in a million years do anything to hurt him or this administration. Clay, I want to continue in my job and serve. I have so much to learn from you and my other colleagues, and I also have so much to give. I don't want to ruin this tremendous opportunity to serve. Plus, we just moved our entire home and family here and are settled in Manassas. I can't go backwards because of my stupid wayward teenage decisions."

He nodded in understanding. "I'll discuss what you told me with White House Counsel. Although I can't determine the outcome, I'll do my best to advocate on your behalf. Let me assure you that in the end, the Secret Service can make a recommendation, but White House Counsel will have the last word on your clearance."

I briefly squeezed my eyes shut. "Thank you, Clay."

He smiled. "It's good you came to me first. This was wise and the right decision."

I went home that night and cried in David's arms. We prayed together, hoping and believing that the outcome would be positive. We waited for what seemed like an eternity.

A few days later, I was called into White House Counsel's office by one of the top-ranking deputies. When I arrived, the deputy counsel was holding my thick file in his lap. "Mrs. Contreras," he started, his eyes staring into mine, "the Secret Service briefed me on your case. It's clear to us that the girl described in this file is not the same mature lady sitting in front of us today. The President's Counsel and I, along with Clay, have confidence in you."

I knew the person serving in the White House Counsel from when we had both worked for the State of Texas under Governor Bush. He was familiar with me and my reputation of getting things done. He said, "We know you have a record of serving Governor Bush for six years. We know you do good work, and Clay vouches for your record and credibility, so that's good enough for us.

Congratulations on your work, Mrs. Contreras. I plan to recommend you full clearance." He smiled and lowered his voice. "And Mrs. Contreras, please consider that as long as you are serving POTUS in the White House, you should not be telling people of your past. I realize you're proud of your transformation, but not everyone will understand you're not the same person. So, I recommend that as long as you work here, you stay the course and keep those intimate details of your past to yourself."

"Yes sir, and duly noted." I turned and walked out of that office with my head held high, knowing that a major miracle had just transpired. I had seen many people disappear after just weeks or a month on the job because they didn't make clearance due to something or another on their record. Thankfully, God spared mine from being tarnished. Plus, I had established a proven record of trust when serving Bush as governor.

I was grateful that David had taken such a firm stand on cutting off ties with Juan early on in our marriage and that my early teen association with him didn't harm my ability to get a clearance. One thing was crystal clear to me—I would not only make it, but I would also thrive in the role! A *major* confidence booster to my spirit.

I now had a new skip in my step. Once again, my visionary husband, my forever knight in shining armor, came to my rescue. Once again, he stood by me, took charge, and wisely counseled me on what to do and how things were going to pan out. And once again, he was right!

Later, I was told that if the Secret Service had come to White House Counsel first without Clay coming forward to share my story, the outcome would have likely turned out very differently. I have lived my adult life and spent my career employing a consistent method of transparency and honesty. It is always the best recipe for overall success.

ANOTHER HURDLE TO CLIMB

Getting my clearance was no small feat, but neither was becoming acclimated to my job and DC. To make matters worse, I was regularly reminded by some in the White House staff that I was the first person in my role without any prior political experience.

Apparently, the presidential appointments portfolio I managed required political savvy. I knew personnel like the back of my hand. I knew Clay's and POTUS's style of management and thus had a sense of ideal profiles of those to serve in the administration, and I certainly knew how to research what I didn't know. But political savvy, I had none. Up until that point in my career, none had been required.

So imagine my surprise when a major political supporter called and complained about me to the White House chief of staff for taking him through the traditional job and board appointments interview process. He had asked, "Doesn't she know who I am?"

Well, I didn't. My lack of political experience prevented me from recognizing his particularly important status or past political relationship to the president. Apparently, I was supposed to know that we give those big boys a bit of special treatment.

Clay called to notify me of the complaint. I was mortified. First of all, should I have known who he was? Secondly, did I do something wrong?

"Clay, I apologize," I said. "I'm still learning all the ins and outs of this DC stuff. I had no idea who he was or that I was supposed to give him special treatment."

"Rebecca," Clay responded, "I want you to know that POTUS and I have full confidence in you. We didn't hire you because you know all the political stuff; we hired you because you know the president and you know personnel. We want you to do the right thing and make recommendations based on merit and experience and not mere political contributions. Let the political office worry about the politics of things, and you keep doing what you're doing."

I was both shocked and thankful that he stood up for me. In that instant, I grew about another ten feet in my confidence. From then on, every time I found myself in a difficult or challenging situation, Clay's belief in me gave me the self-assurance to press on, something I would surely need as I was finally able to go into the Oval Office for my first briefing.

From then on, I started asking my more politically savvy colleagues to show me the ropes so I would not step into it again.

FIRST TIME IN THE OVAL OFFICE

In late March, my colleagues had been meeting with POTUS once a week for over two months to personally brief him on recommended hires for various personnel appointments. Clay wanted me to see the team in action prior to my first briefing opportunity, so he invited me to observe their presentations.

I was filled with complete wonder the first time I walked into the Oval Office with my six colleagues and Clay. The history that has happened in that one room would cause anyone to be filled with respect for the office of the president, no matter their party affiliation or who had been elected.

I didn't know what to expect, so I took cues from my colleagues. They sat on the couch; I sat on the couch. Then in walked President Bush and Vice President Cheney, something I had only watched on TV news, but here I was experiencing it firsthand with such admiration. Everyone stood until the president sat down, and then we all sat down after him. Each person presented their recommendations one by one. When they were done, eyes that belonged to the most powerful people on this planet were all staring at *me*!

Fear overwhelmed me, and my stomach started churning as I glanced around the room and found the vice president of the United States watching me and waiting for me—for *me*—to speak. Suddenly, I flashed back to my past. It was all I could do to keep from squirming as my feelings of inadequacy reminded me of just how unqualified I was for this job. Although I had worked extremely hard to overcome fear and insecurity, I still struggled with both deep down because of my past and lack of formal education. Frequently, I had to pinch myself, given the success I experienced, wondering if one day something would happen, and I would wake up and realize it was all a dream.

Then Clay spoke, thankfully taking their attention off me. "Mr. Vice President Cheney, you haven't met Rebecca yet. She's going to be managing the boards and commission portfolio in PPO. Rebecca is the last person to join our team. She came with us from Texas, and she used to be Governor Bush's HR director."

Before the vice president could respond, President Bush chimed in. "And she's the best damn HR director in Texas. Welcome, Becca, I'm glad you're on the team."

Every single bit of fear, doubt, and weariness melted away in that moment. From then on, I stopped doubting my ability to do the job and held my head high, knowing that whatever I lacked in knowledge or experience didn't matter because Clay had confidence in me and now the president of the United States had personally expressed confidence in me. In turn, I committed right then and there to work around the clock to learn the position and show them both that I could achieve my goals and do a great job.

That briefing did more for me than bolster my self-esteem. Up until then, I just couldn't seem to fit in with some of my colleagues. They had all arrived many weeks before me and were already working together as a seamless presidential personnel team. It was like I had come to the party late.

One particular colleague was perceived as the group's queen bee in terms of her experience in DC. She had worked for Dick Armey on Capitol Hill, and everyone relied on her experience. I had been trying to make friends with her and would have loved for her to take me under her wing and show me a thing or two about DC, the White House, and my job. But she was extremely busy, just like the rest of the team, so all my attempts to get her to mentor me failed.

But on that day as we were leaving the Oval Office, she turned to me with a big smile. "Oh my God, POTUS really loves you, Rebecca." No longer was I an outsider as she brought me into her inner circle. Over the years, as we continued to work together at the White House, I grew close to her and gained her trust. She was incredibly smart, and I learned a lot from just watching her in action.

I also set out to break every record in the boards and commissions portfolio—and I accomplished my goal!

DAVID GETS A JOB IN THE ADMINISTRATION

We were about three months in, and David had not been able to secure a job yet in the tech industry. When we left Texas, Applied Materials indicated they had a fabrication plant where they made microchips ten minutes from where we were going to live. We were sure that David would easily get a job there. After all, they had just hired him and wanted to keep him on board.

He then found out the hours were unrealistic. I was already working seven days a week, fourteen-hour days, and we agreed that there was no way he could pull long hours as well. He needed to have the steady, flexible schedule so that one of us was there for the children, especially because we had no family in the area to provide that support.

He turned that job down and started his hunt for another job. The clock was ticking as we had our new large mortgage—twice the amount of our Texas mortgage—coming due. Thankfully, we had secured a tenant to lease our home in Austin, so that at least was covered. After knocking on many doors, he seemed to hit one brick wall after another. Then during a conversation with friends at dinner in our new home in Manassas, they asked David where he was working.

"Well, nowhere right now," he answered, "but I would love to work for the president one day if I could."

I charged back, "You can't work for the president! I work for the president, and we can't both work in the administration."

He told me later that my comment cut him down about two sizes. I explained that it was not practical for him to also get a job in the administration. Plus, I wasn't going to use my position to help him. I felt strongly that it was unethical to use my job for our personal gain and told him he was on his own.

Later that month in March 2001, David was invited to an event in the Organization of American States. POTUS was having a summit with all the ambassadors from Latin America, and about 300 people were expected to attend. David accepted the invitation, and I agreed to try to meet him if my schedule allowed. I was mindful that White House rules cautioned employees about attending too many public events on White House time, but since this one happened to fall within my lunch hour, it worked out perfectly. It would be the first event my husband and I attended together as a couple since the inauguration activities in January.

Afterward, as we were getting up to leave, the Secret Service shut everything down and said, "No ma'am, the president will be making his way out to the lobby to greet the dignitaries right after he speaks, so no one can leave right now."

We sat back down to wait it out. Within minutes, another Secret Service agent came and asked us to follow him. We had no idea where we were going or what was happening until it was too late. We didn't realize we were seated in the section reserved for dignitaries. As a result, we were being escorted to the receiving line to greet POTUS.

I about passed out from anxiety. I could not be seen standing in the receiving line for dignitaries. David was tickled pink that he would get to personally say hello to the president and asked me to calm down. David had not had a chance to talk with him since he had hosted the 1999 Christmas party for his team and their families in the Governor's Mansion. So David was very excited to be up close and personal with now President Bush.

I pleaded with the Secret Service agent to please let me out of the line, to let me stand in the back. He firmly stated, "Ma'am, you're not going anywhere. The president will be here any minute. No one moves."

I just stood there speechless, cringing at the thought of my big boss seeing me amid the dignitaries. The line formed in a big oval shape with about twenty people. Before we knew it, POTUS was making his way down the line doing "grip and grin" greetings, staying no more than two or three seconds per guest to move quickly. The White House photographer followed him, snapping pictures as he greeted each dignitary. When he saw me, he reached over to give me a hug and kiss on the cheek. "Becca, good to see you."

Whew! I wasn't in trouble after all. Relief flooded through my mind!

He went on to the next person and then returned to David, even though he still had other people to greet. "David, how are you?" he asked. "I want to personally thank you for allowing Rebecca to work for me. She's doing a great job in Presidential Personnel. Thank you for moving your family all the way up here to serve in the administration."

I was stunned that he was thanking *us*.

Then he asked David, "What are you doing here?"

"Mr. President, well, I came to hear you speak today."

"No, I mean what are you doing here in DC for a job? Have you gotten a job yet?"

"Well, I'm knocking on doors, sir. I still haven't found a job yet, but I'll keep knocking."

The president pointed at me and said, "Well, Rebecca does personnel, you know. She should be able to help you." Then he turned to me and said, "Rebecca, help him please."

No joke!

That night, it was all David could talk about. "The president said you need to help me. Take my resumé in and put it in the stack of 90,000 applicants so at least I'm in the stack."

I adamantly shook my head. "Nope. Not going to do that. I'm not going to use my job to get you a job. You need to do it on your own."

The next week at the end of the Oval Office briefing, POTUS remembered that encounter with David. "Becca, has David found a job yet?" he asked. "You tell me when he does, okay?"

"Yes sir, I will, but he's still looking."

He did that a couple more times until one day, my colleague Dina turned to me and said, "Wow, POTUS really seems concerned about David. Maybe I should interview him and see if he's a fit at one of my agencies. There might be a job for him at SBA (Small Business Administration)."

I shrugged. "Sure, if you want to, call him."

Within three weeks of that conversation, she hired David for a Schedule C Presidential appointment, and he started his job at SBA in April 2001. Schedule C jobs are mid-tier to senior-level jobs in the administration that can be appointed by agency heads and do not require senate confirmation or presidential signature. Generally, those jobs are handled via direct appointment by Presidential Personnel staff.

Just weeks later, David got to personally tell POTUS in another Marine One arrival ceremony that he had indeed secured a job and was working for him. President Bush smiled and said, "Welcome aboard. Congratulations! Glad you're on the team."

Little did we know that when we made that leap of faith to Washington DC and David left his ten-year career in the tech industry, he would also have an opportunity to serve the president. It's amazing how things align and work out for the greater good! Once again, it speaks to the incredible care President Bush personally had for my family. There are many stories and encounters like mine where he took personal care of the people who served in his administration, and how he genuinely loved his people. This kind of true, honest, and caring leadership is rare, and I'm just thankful that David and I both got to experience it in action.

David served for the entire first term of the administration in two roles, first as special liaison at the Small Business Administration, then as deputy director for the President's Faith-based Initiative at the Department of Housing and Urban Development.

Since we both worked in DC then, we spent many hours on the commute from Manassas to downtown DC, about two hours per day, talking about our dreams, sharing our day, and finding time to sharpen one another and encourage each other in our journeys.

DAVID BY MY SIDE

The beauty of David's new job was the flexibility he had with his schedule. He was able to work out a four-day workweek with an early start to ensure that he had three solid days with the kids. After a while, he was able to alternate his schedule to be off every-other Monday, a perfect way to augment my insane schedule so that he could be present with our family.

Since we were both in the administration, we were able to attend most events together and came to be known as a power couple in DC. Photos of those events are featured in this book: the Kennedy Honors Awards, the National Art Museum Annual Gala, red carpet events for various blockbuster movie premiers, the annual spring and summer galas for the U.S. Hispanic Chamber of Commerce, dinners at various embassies, congressional galas, and others.

Since I was a top-ranking commissioned officer of Hispanic decent, I was often asked to give a keynote address as a surrogate for POTUS for some of the national Hispanic events. David was able to attend with me, providing the full support and encouragement I needed. Most of those events were quite intimidating due to the sheer size of the crowds, which, in most cases, consisted of thousands of attendees. Having my husband by my side certainly helped me get my sea legs in public speaking, a skill that has come in quite handy today.

I am incredibly thankful to POTUS, my boss Clay, and to my colleague Dina who all gave us the opportunity to experience that journey together. It is rare that a husband-and-wife team both get to work for a president at the same time.

FAMILY VISIT TO THE WHITE HOUSE LAWN FOR PRESIDENTIAL ARRIVAL

President George W. Bush is a family man, and that trait poured over onto his staff and their families. During my tenure at the White House, so many memories were made for my family. One was the historic one-hundred-year traditional Easter Egg Roll on the White House lawn in April 2001.

In the beginning, Crystaline sure didn't feel like making memories. She wasn't acclimating to DC. Instead, she was acting out for attention and making poor choices, and I was concerned about her. POTUS often asked about my family, and once he asked specifically about how Crystaline was doing in her transition. He remembered her, that she was now in middle school, and was aware that other children from his transition team around Crystaline's age were struggling with the move, thus his concern.

I answered, "Mr. President, I'm having a really tough time with her. She doesn't understand why we're here and honestly doesn't want to be here. I'm at a crossroads, and if I don't start seeing some positive changes in her, I might have to reconsider my role in the White House."

He nodded in understanding. "As you know, I'm a father of two daughters myself." He paused. "Hey, the next time there's an arrival, why don't you bring Crystaline to me so I can talk with her?"

An arrival is when the Marine One helicopter returns POTUS and, at times, the first family, to the White House grounds. Arrivals were only open to White House staff and their guests, who lined up and waited to wave from a distance as they welcomed the president or first family. On occasion, POTUS would walk over to the line to say hello. Most of the time, though, he and Mrs. Bush would just wave from a distance.

Sure enough, there was a Marine One arrival from Camp David about a month later. For this arrival, there must have been a hundred people present. My family got there early, so we stood in the front row. President Bush and Mrs. Bush walked out of Marine One and darted straight toward my family.

POTUS stood in front of Crystaline, and both he and his wife greeted her and my son, Caleb, by name. Their ability to always remember my family member's names still amazes me. Thousands of people worked for them, five hundred alone in the White House, yet they took the time to remember the names of my family.

He said, "Crystaline, I want to thank you for allowing your mom to do what she does for me. She has a really important job." He then asked her about school and how she was doing. It was incredible how he also remembered our conversation from a month before and made a personal point to reach out to my daughter.

We went home and talked about mom's and dad's important jobs for the president. Although she was only in eighth grade and couldn't see the bigger picture yet, she seemed to understand we had a job to do.

After that incident, I saw a difference in her.

Fortunately, it was a lesson she learned just in time. Crystaline would be tested, as would the rest of the world, when right around the corner, we'd all experience a day that would rock this country and forever change history.

CHAPTER SIX

OUR WORLD CHANGED FOREVER

"Every heart we touch, decision we make, and action we take creates the legacy we live and leave behind. That legacy brings people to you who match your energy. It's magnetic and it keeps attracting more of the same."

—SHARON LECHTER

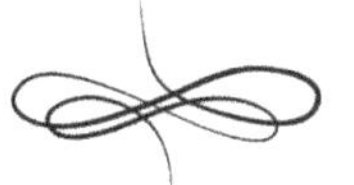

I'll never forget that morning, where I was, what I was doing. Yet it started out like any other beautiful and clear day in DC, belying what was to come.

As I walked out of our house for our drive to work, the spectacular backdrop of blue skies with white billowing clouds greeted me with the promise of a beautiful day. Soon, we'd be experiencing our first fall in Washington DC. After all, it was already September 11.

I climbed into the passenger seat of our vehicle while David got into the driver's seat. Since we both worked for the administration, we had been carpooling since mid-April. He drove the whole way until we were about half a block from the White House. Then he pulled over and stopped, got out, and walked to the nearest metro station to finish his trip to the SBA. I got behind the wheel and finished my trip to the White House complex, where free parking was one of my perks as a White House commissioned officer. Free parking in DC was coveted as fees can be up to fifty dollars per day, and the government doesn't reimburse their employees for parking.

I walked to my office in the Old Executive Office Building. After grabbing my coffee, I sat down at my desk and gazed out of the spectacular large window that overlooked the West Wing and White House lawn area where the press corps was set up. Behind me was a TV that stayed muted unless there was a live press conference or other POTUS-related coverage on the news.

It was also the first day of the White House internship program. Three new interns had been assigned to our team as we were still in the middle of sourcing candidates for appointments to various boards and commissions.

Around 9:15, I heard a scurry outside my window. Hundreds of people were running out of the White House and West Wing and across the White House lawn.

Ladies were holding their shoes, running like they were being chased. Those who chose to run with their heels on were tripping and falling.

I peered into the hallway to see what was happening and saw hundreds of people evacuating. The Secret Service came into my office and started yelling, "Get out of here. Now!"

Their unprecedented demeanor startled me more. I grabbed my things and found my team in the office next to mine. They were also grabbing their stuff while the Secret Service agents now yelled, "We have to get out! Two planes have hit the twin towers in New York City, and they think it's a terrorist attack. One's coming here to the White House, so everyone's being evacuated!"

The interns and one of my junior staff members were crying, so I immediately kicked into "mama mode." Amid the turmoil, I needed to calm them down and get my team out. We all assembled as a group and left the building.

A Secret Service agent spotted me. "Mrs. Contreras, we've been instructed to escort you to a secret undisclosed location. You must come with us now."

Glancing around at the distressed faces before me, I responded, "I don't want to leave my team, and I've got to call my husband; he's over by the Capitol. We have kids at home in Manassas."

Firmly and respectfully, he stated, "Mrs. Contreras, I must insist you come with me now. Please let me do my job."

When we arrived at the secure multilevel row house in Georgetown, I recognized my colleagues. In sheer horror, we watched over and over the video of the planes hitting the towers. Then we watched as each of the buildings collapsed.

My heart sank with pain and fear as I struggled with my thoughts. The events taking place in New York were surreal, and I was now in a potential target zone?

At 9:37 a.m., the unaccounted-for American Airlines Flight 77 now appeared and slammed into the Pentagon just across the Potomac River from us! Tucked away in this secure location, I could only imagine the pandemonium and panic the city was experiencing. The Pentagon was attacked. Now the cell towers had been shut down to keep the terrorists, who were trying to attack DC, from communicating with each other. But the efforts also severed communication for everyone else. I was isolated from the outside world, consumed with thoughts about my family. My kids probably heard about an attack in the District and would be worried about their parents, yet I had no way to let them know I was okay. Furthermore, how was I going to get home to them thirty miles away?

What about David? Was he okay? I had no way to reach him. And if I couldn't reach him, then how I was going to even find him? He worked by the US Capitol, and was that building also a target? All these questions circling in my head.

I tried to put my focus onto something else. Right now, I had no control of the situation, and obsessing about it was going to increase my anxiety level even higher. So, I took the action steps I had learned in the past to calm my emotions down and kept a close eye on the news and any updates.

I was shocked and saddened to see that at 10:03 a.m., another plane crashed, this time in Pennsylvania. Was it headed for us? Was there another plane delegated to crash? Where? The lack of knowing was almost paralyzing. I wanted, needed to be with my husband and kids.

We still didn't have any cell phone service. David would be frantic and do whatever he needed to do to find me and get us home to our kids.

For now, though, it appeared I wasn't going anywhere. The chief of staff had given special orders to keep the president's top team out of harm's way. This meant not letting us out of our holding area until cleared by the Secret Service. So, I continued waiting in agony and racking my brain on what to do to reach David.

Then several of us joined hands and began praying for the situation. Within ten minutes, a miracle happened. My BlackBerry rang from a number with a 713-area code—Manassas. I snatched it up and couldn't answer it fast enough. It was my neighbor Shirley. "Rebecca? Are you okay?"

"Yes, I'm fine. Have you heard from the kids?"

"We have Crystaline, but Caleb's still in school. They're keeping the younger kids there because so many parents are picking them up. Once his school lets out, the buses will take the remaining kids home. When he arrives, we'll go and get him. You just get home when you can and don't worry about them."

I let out a big sigh of relief. God sent angels, those neighbors of ours. Still, I was worried; Caleb was not with his sister or any other family member or friend.

I asked if she knew anything about David. Shirley said that neither she nor Sheila, another neighbor, had been able to reach him so far. "It's just a wonder I was able to get ahold of you at all," she declared.

Then I heard Sheila in the background. Shirley exclaimed, "Oh my gosh! Sheila just came in the door. She says she has David on her cell phone!"

My heart raced with excitement. He must be okay if he was talking to Sheila. I found it miraculous that our phones were working when all communication had been shut down, and that one neighbor had me on the phone and the other had David on the phone at the same time.

Shirley announced, "Sheila says that David's been walking around the White House perimeter for two hours looking for you. What do you want me to tell him about where to meet you?"

They passed instructions back and forth.

David told Sheila, "Have Rebecca meet me at George Washington Hospital. That's close to where she is if she's in downtown Georgetown."

I confirmed his instructions through our neighbors. Then the line went dead again. Strangely, our phones only worked for a few minutes, which was just long enough to make our plans to meet. Afterward, we didn't get a signal again the whole time we were in DC.

Hope had been infused! Both children and my husband were all fine. Plus, David had a plan to reunite, and his plans always worked!

I thanked God for answering my questions and for protecting us all. Then I told my colleagues I was stepping out to get some fresh air, which I truly needed, and snuck away.

The White House complex was quite large, and I often had to walk between its three different buildings that were blocks away from each other. Wearing heels was painful, so I always carried my running shoes in my bag. Well, I put them on and ran for about twenty minutes like a professional runner all the way to Georgetown Hospital.

The chaos had intensified. The clear blue skies were now filled with thick black smoke billowing out from the Pentagon as the fires continued to burn from the terrorist attack. F-16 fighter jets blazed overhead, their sound piercing into the chaos. Traffic was backed up as far as the eye could see. Sirens were blaring, and cars were blowing their horns at the hordes of people clogging the streets in their attempts to find safety.

As I approached the hospital, I could see David standing on a brick wall as though perched on a lookout tower. With tears streaming down my face at the sight of him, I sprinted with a new surge of energy until we were able to grab each other as if we were just rescued from a sinking ship.

Our next goal was to figure out how we were going to get home to our kids. It was about 1:00 p.m., and no one was allowed back in the White House complex, so we couldn't get our vehicle from the parking lot. There was no cab service, and hundreds of thousands of people were trying to get out of DC all at once. In my mind, there was no solution.

However, David brought the solution with him. One of his SBA colleagues was older, alone, and afraid, so she came along with David. She announced, "They've shut down most of the metro lines, but the orange line's still running to Vienna. My car's parked there, and since Manassas is close by, I can give you a ride home."

So, we jumped on the orange line and headed to Vienna!

When we finally got home at nearly 3:00 p.m., Crystaline was waiting outside on the neighbor's porch. As soon as she saw us, she ran toward us and hugged us.

Through her sobs, she said, "I thought you both were dead. They told us at school a plane was headed to the White House." Her teacher forgot that I worked in the White House when she irresponsibly announced that news to the class without thinking about Crystaline. She continued, "I immediately prayed and asked God to please be with my dad and my mom. But I was prepared to take care of Caleb if anything did happen to you. He's still not here. We're waiting for the bus to bring him home."

In that moment, Crystaline grew years in maturity, and her natural-born leadership instincts kicked in.

We went inside our home and turned on the TV. The full video coverages of the terrorist attacks were displayed on the screen. It was the first time we had been able to see all of it, and we sat in disbelief.

Shortly afterward, Caleb walked into the house. I immediately grabbed him, thankful he was safe, and then I held him tight. He had no clue what was going on. He told us that all the parents came and picked up all the kids at his school, but he and four others were left at the school for the rest of the day.

I finally let him go and then encouraged him to go play outside with his friends. Thinking he was too young to fully understand, we didn't want him to watch the TV.

When the Pentagon fires came on, I flashed back to how just one month ago in that very building I was having a private lunch with the Secretary of Army's special advisor to better understand West Point Military Academy. It was one of the boards I was in charge of, and I needed to make solid recommendations to POTUS. I was then taken on a tour of the Pentagon and walked through West Point's overall strategy and goals to determine the types of people who would be ideal board members.

Then I thought, *What if I had been in the building today?*

I was also concerned for the Pentagon team and their safety. Clearly, many lives were lost, both in the plane and on the ground, but at that time it was hard to tell. By some miracle, however, the Pentagon wing the terrorists hit was under construction and therefore mostly empty. I couldn't imagine the damage and how many more people would have died if the wing had been fully occupied.

In the middle of processing these horrific sights, the home phone kept ringing off the hook, and David stepped in to handle all the calls with family, friends, and even an Austin news station that had heard we were in DC.

Exhausted physically and emotionally, all I could do was collapse on the couch. But before I could pass out, Caleb rushed in from outside. He stared at the TV for about a minute before turning to David and proclaiming, "Dad, when I grow up, I'm going to become an architect and rebuild those towers, okay? Okay, bye, Dad. I'm going back outside to play again."

We were both in awe of the perspective of an innocent child. Such hope, such promise…

I faded in and out of sleep for about two hours and then faintly heard David in the background still talking on the phone. When I woke up, I had missed a call on my BlackBerry from Clay. He left a message informing me that POTUS's instructions were for us all to get back to work at the White House the next morning. His direction was clear: we were not going to let the terrorists disturb our work or mission—period. Bright and early the next morning, I returned to the White House, and David returned to his job at SBA.

BACK TO THE WHITE HOUSE

Our Oval Office meetings were scaled back to twice a month and shortened from a full hour to thirty to forty-five minutes. So, two weeks to the day of the 9/11 tragedy, I was back in the Oval Office with my colleagues for our personnel meeting with POTUS.

All of us were shocked. We weren't sure what we should say to him or how we should approach our meeting. To me, our work was insignificant compared to the post-9/11 issues he was dealing with. I asked Clay, "How do I talk with him given all he has on his plate?"

He responded to all of us, "Just like you did before. Nothing is changing. We all still have a job to do, and he expects us to keep doing it the same way we've been doing it."

We walked in, sat down, and waited for POTUS to come into the office. This time, Vice President Cheney wasn't with him, which up until that day wasn't normal. He had attended most of our early personnel meetings because some of the appointments were for the Department of Defense, and that was an area of interest to him. We were told that the president and vice president were not to be in the same meetings to ensure continuity of government if anything happened.

When President Bush walked in, we all stood, and he motioned for us to sit down. My colleague Jodey, who we had hired back in 1995 from the internship program under then-Governor Bush, had been co-leading the White House Bible study group. He said, "Mr. President, we want you to know we're all praying for you."

I added, "Mr. President, yes, please know you are covered in our prayers daily. We love you."

He responded, "Please continue to pray. We all need God's wisdom and help through this difficult time. I also want to thank you for coming back to the White House. I know you all have families, and I want you to know I appreciate what you do."

Wow. Here he was once again thanking us.

"Okay, let's get started," he said, and Clay jumped right in to lead the meeting. It turned out to be great.

When we walked out, I had a lump in my throat. I went into the bathroom, fell on my knees, and cried, intently praying to God to be with our president. I also thanked God for the honor and opportunity He had blessed me with to be a part of this man's team.

Most impressive during that tremendous crisis was President Bush's focus and resolve. Nothing, and I mean nothing, shook our great leader or distracted him from what he firmly believed needed to be his response in leading our great country. He wasn't swayed by what had happened on 9/11. He wasn't swayed by public opinion. How I learned from him that day and the days that followed.

How we need that in America today.

PROMOTIONS IN THE AIR

The cleanup of 9/11's mass destruction began, but the grief for lost loved ones would never end. The country we once knew was gone as a feeling of vulnerability swept across it from the east coast to the west.

My family had been shaken, but we stood firm. Here in the DC area, as far as family goes, we only had each other. Consequently, we became closer, appreciating every day we were given. Frankly, though, we were homesick. We missed our family and the things we did with them. We missed the simple, normal (and affordable) life that might have seemed hectic at the time but looking back was pretty good. What happened on 9/11 made us miss home that much more.

Our life in Austin was a large part of our early foundation, so in a sense, this separation felt like our footing had been kicked out from under us. It didn't help that some of our loved ones didn't support our decision to join the Bush administration and serve our country. They couldn't understand why we couldn't just be happy with what we had. One family member even accused us of accepting these jobs to further ourselves and our careers at the cost of uprooting our children and moving them across the country. Funny how others can't tell the difference at times between service-centered and opportunity-focused decisions.

I wondered, if these naysayers spent one week in our shoes, would they still have the same misperception? First, our commute in DC was insane. A thirty-mile trip that would take thirty to forty-five minutes in Austin often took up to two hours due to the incredible traffic where three major areas—Maryland, Virginia, and DC—merged. To arrive to work by 8:30 a.m., we'd have to leave the house by 6:30 a.m. We'd get off work at 5:30 p.m. and, if we were lucky, arrive home by 7:00 or 7:30. Although our days were long and exhausting at times, we kept pushing forward, realizing and acknowledging that we were given a once-in-a-lifetime chance to serve our country by working for not just any president, but for President George W. Bush.

Frequently, my role as a commissioned officer and surrogate of the president required me to represent him at numerous evening events that usually required fancy dresses and tuxedos. Because we had children, David and I were very selective about which events we attended and how many nights out we could do. We made two firm commitments—first, we would do our best to ensure 100 percent of our weekends were all about family. So, we'd often decline any of those requests that required a Saturday or Sunday attendance. Second, whatever events we attended, we would attend as a couple or not at all. Fortunately, Crystaline was now in high school, so she would babysit Caleb, which allowed us to stay in DC and attend various important events and galas.

After two years of serving POTUS in the White House, I had completed my boards and commission portfolio (1,200 positions strong). Not only did our team break records in working through the entire large-scale portfolio in just two years as opposed to the usual four, but we fulfilled POTUS's desire to have one of the most diverse set of appointments in the history of the White House Presidential Personnel Office (PPO) team, something we were all immensely proud of. I knew then that although I loved my perks from working inside the White House, in order for me to continue to grow and learn, I had to get outside the walls of its compound and into a government agency where, as my boss would declare, "the real work is done for the American taxpayers."

By April 2003, I was up for a new challenge, and three possibilities presented themselves—working for Secretary Colin Powell at the U.S. State Department, serving Secretary John Snow as an HR director for the U.S. Department of Treasury, or serving in the role of U.S. Treasurer.

I was thrilled that numerous options were on the table. Now I needed to ensure that I was positioned to best continue to serve POTUS and achieve my long-term career goals. I'm a firm believer that every step you take leads to the next step, and our ability to impact those around us is greatly influenced by those steps we take. Most important was my ability to move into a new role that afforded me the opportunity to make a difference.

I needed to talk with Clay. He had moved from Presidential Personnel to the deputy director for management of the Office of Management and Budget (OMB). He was leading the President's Management Agenda (PMA), President Bush's signature initiative for management reform in the federal government. Clay became widely known as the "management guru" in government.

In the meantime, I spoke with his replacement in White House PPO, a former colleague of mine who knew me and the quality of my work. Her suggestion was that I consider the U.S. Treasurer position. She had indicated that the treasurer was leaving, and she wanted to recommend someone that the president knew who could represent him with pride.

I was once again blown away and incredibly humbled that my name had surfaced for this prestigious role. Lots of exceptionally smart people worked in the administration, so the competition was stiff. Bear in mind, when vacancies of this magnitude occur, there's usually a process in place for numerous top officials to vet candidates over several weeks.

One thing I've learned in my career and life is to not always jump at the first chance but evaluate all factors, seek counsel, and make sure the launching point is right. The position of treasurer would have taken me completely out of my area of expertise in HR and public speaking, requiring me to travel about 50 percent of the time. I felt a bit unqualified, but she felt I should consider it and that I could learn the role and job.

I took her suggestion under advisement and subsequently met with Clay to get his counsel. When I presented my options to him, he said, "No doubt, you need to consider the Treasury HR job. Treasury's in the midst of numerous HR and management challenges, and you're just the person to tackle them head-on." He shared that the opportunity was ripe for impact and change, and he further believed that the U.S. Treasurer role was highly ceremonial in nature. Although it might sound fun to have my name printed on U.S. currency, Clay said it wasn't the best use of my talent and service to the president. Leave it to Clay to always deliver the bottom line with no nonsense!

His suggestion felt right, though. I loved the idea of getting back to the core of my HR roots. The U.S. Treasury Department would be the largest portfolio I had ever managed, with approximately 128,000 employees. Eight subagencies were inside the Department's oversight, each with their own human resource director. However, I would go in as a presidential appointee with the authority and support from the White House to affect much-needed changes at Treasury with the President's Management Agenda. The effective management and execution of HR was one of the central tenants measured under this reform initiative. According to Clay, Treasury's President's Management Agenda scorecard at the time was red, which was failing. It was crucial that it be pulled up and past yellow to a green rating.

A few weeks later, I moved to Treasury to assume the top executive government position in the appointed role of deputy assistant secretary and chief human capital officer, a mouthful on its own. Then in May 2003, I accepted a non-senate-confirmed presidential appointment to the head of HR at the U.S. Treasury. The former title was so long that we decided to call it "CHCO" (short for chief human capital officer). Congress had just implemented legislative reform instituting a new CHCO Council shortly before I took on the role. I would be the first Treasury CHCO assigned to the federal council led by the director of Federal Office of Personnel or OPM.

I later learned I was one of fifteen CHCOs appointed to the new congressionally mandated council. The CHCO's primary responsibility was to advise POTUS and Congress on necessary government-wide HR reforms.

My first meeting for the CHCO Council was held at OPM in a large ornate room with a beautiful horseshoe-shaped mahogany table that sat about twenty people. Each placement had a nameplate and microphone for the official public meetings and hearings where we would have to discuss important HR reforms. Additionally, my new role as Treasury's CHCO was to bring all the ten-plus agency HR directors together under one roof and help negotiate and advocate management and reform across the whole department. In essence, my Treasury HQ office was the "policy shop" and executive oversight organization that impacted all HR offices and programs across the Department of Treasury.

This new position is the sole reason I now have my consulting firm, AvantGarde. The incredible experiences, initiatives, and reforms I supported and implemented, as well as the network I built doing it, paved the way for my long-term career of starting and building a thriving government consulting practice.

FAVOR AND PROMOTIONS CONTINUE

During the same time period I was leaving the White House, David was also asked to take on bigger and better responsibilities. He had successfully performed his role at SBA and was asked to serve as deputy director in the President's Faith-based Office at the Department of Housing and Urban Development (HUD). He accepted with great enthusiasm because the whole time he worked at SBA, he had to wanted serve in this faith-based initiative. I love the fact that two years later, he was afforded that opportunity all due to his good work at SBA.

David experienced the tremendous impact of the initiative on nonprofits all over America. He even got to travel with POTUS to the Los Angeles Dream Center to see firsthand how some of the nonprofits' hard work were transforming lives, especially those of inner-city youth. POTUS called these nonprofits "armies of compassion." On many occasions, you'd hear President Bush say, "Government can lend a hand, but only God can change a heart." The Faith-based Initiative was his signature program that allowed his words to be put into action. It removed the red tape that had been preventing good solid 501(c)3 organizations from applying for and getting government-funded grants. He believed that certified 501(c)3 organizations that were rehabilitating drug addicts, helping with prison reform, feeding and clothing the homeless, or training inner-city kids via GED programs or vocational training should not be discriminated against just because they identified as faith based. They should all be eligible for the same federal dollars as any other.

David's experiences prompted him to start envisioning our own nonprofit. He was still just as passionate about helping inner-city youth as he was when we first met. So in 2004, he began to write that vision down. He said, "It may be time to start thinking about investing our own time, talent, and treasure into giving back to our inner-city communities in Austin." We spent many evenings talking about the possibility and the what-ifs.

In the meantime, we continued to serve to the best of our abilities in positions we could have only dreamed about ten years earlier. With each moment, we took in as much as we could to learn and expand our knowledge, experience, and portfolios.

OUR WORLD ROCKED BY NEWS FROM MOM

In the fall of 2004, we visited my mom. While there, she asked me to look at a lump on her breast that had been causing her pain for about a year. Her words worried me, so we went into the bathroom so that I could see what she was talking about. She showed me the lump, and I was shocked to see it was the size of a grapefruit and had engorged her entire breast.

The emotions overwhelmed me, and I wrapped my arms around her. Together, we cried there in the bathroom. "Mom," I asked her in a pleading tone, "why didn't you tell me? Why haven't you seen a doctor?"

She continued to cry, and I could feel her fear. I had to force her to make an appointment to see a specialist. In the meantime, my job required me to go back to DC because POTUS was in the middle of his reelection campaign. It was difficult to leave her, and the weight of not being there to at least take her to the doctor hit me a ton of bricks on my heart and mind.

Not too long afterwards, I got the phone call. "Rebecca, it's stage 4 breast cancer," she announced. I was devastated. Mom and I had grown quite close over the years.

She began the journey of radiation and chemotherapy. I felt useless to her 1,500 miles away. I could only encourage her, pray with and for her, and continually believe for a miracle, but it wasn't the same as being there.

Maybe David was right about the transition back to Texas. We needed to move back home. I knew Mom; she was a fighter, always had been, but I didn't believe she could go through this battle on her own. I was closest to Mom, and I felt strongly I needed to be by her side, living back in Austin for the next level of her journey, where she would face a giant that I suspected would be incredibly hard to defeat.

BUSH'S REELECTION JOURNEY

About three weeks before the November 2004 presidential election, David decided to use the paid time off he had accumulated and volunteer to go on the reelection campaign trail. I also wanted to volunteer, but realistically only one of us could; someone had to manage the home front. Since David had taken care of everything early in in the first term so I could be in DC, we decided it was my turn to stay home with the kids.

Then after Bush won the presidential election in a landslide against Senator John Kerry, our discussions about our future and our own nonprofit intensified. They were no longer dreams but decisions to be made. David continued to draw out his vision to start the nonprofit. By now, he was convinced that in order to bring it to fruition, we must be back home in "God's country," as we Texans like to call it.

Crystaline helped tip the scales when she announced, "Mom, Dad, I graduate from high school at the end of this school year, and I want to do it in Texas. I want all my family there at my graduation, and I can't do that here in Virginia."

I felt peace with this decision. I wanted to be close to Mom anyway so that I could help her in her battle against breast cancer. She needed me, and I needed to be there for her.

We loved our jobs, DC, and President Bush, and serving the president of the United States had afforded us such tremendous experiences. But they had come at a cost and turned out to be incredibly taxing on our family's schedule. We had been going nonstop, and the demands of the jobs were only increasing because we were being asked to consider bigger jobs in a second term. We had invested in our country, but now it was time to invest in us as a family.

We knew what we now had to do—resign, return home to Austin, resettle, and regroup. Neither of us had a job in place because we wanted to take a few months off to work on us and spend time with our family. Nevertheless, we had a tremendous sense of peace. Whatever was in store for our careers, it would all come together once we moved back home.

Our time in DC was over.

TEXAS, HERE WE COME!

Now that we had made our decision, events took a turn for the good, and all the right pieces fell into place for this big move. To start, we were given notice by our tenants in Round Rock, Texas, that they would be moving out in December 2004. We now had a vacant house.

We put our Manassas home up for sale in a record market, and it sold ten days later for way above market price. David and I walked away with a significant amount of cash in our pockets. We decided to pay off our credit card debt, scale down our expenses, move back into our smaller home in Round Rock, and then take about three months off to rest, recharge, and map out our next steps.

With grateful hearts and a resolved plan, we both submitted our resignations in early December. Our last day would be December 31, 2004. We wanted to personally give POTUS one last goodbye.

The occasion presented itself during the Christmas party for White House staff. When David and I were able to speak to the president, we thanked him for the opportunity to be part of such a tremendous team and told him how proud we were to serve under his leadership. "Mr. President," I said, "I also want to thank you for the most amazing ten years of my life."

When I shared with him that we were going back to Texas, in true Bush form, he jokingly replied, "If I can't go home yet, you can't either."

We all laughed. POTUS thanked us for our service and wished us well. I find it amazing that in all he had going on, he once again was thanking us.

On January 2, 2005, we left for Texas. While driving away from DC, memories flooded my mind…my first day, how nervous yet excited I was, the challenges of adjusting to my job, of my family adjusting to a completely new world, of reuniting after 9/11. I thought about the friendships we had made—some for a season and some who would remain in our lives for years to come. This once-in-a-lifetime venture had been good to us, and we had been good to it.

These thoughts continued for many miles, even after DC's skyline was long gone from my side-view mirror. But we had made the right decision, and my nostalgia turned to excitement as I stopped looking back and started looking forward to what lay ahead.

After driving for two days, we finally crossed the Texas border. We were home, and Crystaline, Caleb, and I were so ecstatic we stuck our heads out of the Tahoe's windows to announce our arrival to the whole world. With the wind pushing against our faces, we yelled at the top of our lungs, "Texas, here we are! So glad to see you!"

The next few months were incredible, with much-needed R&R for our entire family—sleeping in late, David riding bikes to school with Caleb. For the first time ever, both David and I were there to greet the kids when they got home from school. We had snacks ready and would take time to do fun stuff with them. Then during their times off from school, we would take vacations to different places. We were getting closer as a family, making up for lost time. My marriage also got stronger as David and I regrouped and reconnected in many ways, making sure we incorporated our newfound weekly "date nights" consistently. We reconnected with Texas friends, and it was like we had never left.

Then in May 2005, Crystaline got her wish—she walked across the stage to get her diploma in cap and gown, graduating in her home state of Texas! And all of her family was there cheering her on. We were finally back to normal...or so we thought.

CUTTING MY TEETH IN CONSULTING

During our much-needed rest, David and I started putting out feelers for job opportunities. Since I had worked for the government my entire career, my focus was on that industry. My sizeable executive experience would hopefully land me a position in a larger agency.

It didn't take long before employers showed interest in us. David ended up being recruited by the Council on Faith in Action (CONFIA), a local 501c4 organization. CONFIA advocated for a Texas constitutional clause to institute a marriage amendment. It was a heavy grassroots effort among Hispanic churches across Texas, since their communities were the group's target. At the same time, he continued mapping out the plan and curriculum to start our nonprofit, LaunchPad.

I had a few interviews with the governor's office to run the operations for a small agency and with Dell Computers as a potential HR vice president. Although I was excited and the likelihood of my being offered a job at both were high, things just didn't feel right at the time. I really wanted to keep my options open and possibly move into a role where I could learn new things to strengthen my career portfolio.

In mid-March, I received an unsolicited email from a businessman in DC named John. He was referred by a mutual friend from our church in Virginia and had heard about my work with the Chief Human Capital Officer's Council and my federal network. He wanted to start a practice in the federal market, mostly in HR consulting services. He ended his email by writing, "I'd like for you to come to DC to meet with me and talk about joining my firm."

I didn't respond immediately, but he continued to email me, so I eventually wrote back. "Thank you for your interest and email. I'm intrigued, but I'm not going to DC again. If you want to meet, you need to come to Austin."

Within the week or so, he was in Austin! We met over lunch at a hotel near the airport. After a two-hour meeting to explain his vision, he convinced me that I would be an incredible asset to his small HR consulting firm. He gave a great proposal. "If you choose to join my company in DC, I'll make you executive vice president, pay you a good salary, and also pay you a commission on the work you win for the company."

His offer was tempting, but I still had reservations, which I shared with him. "I just moved back from DC. Although I'm honored that you're interested in me for this position, I simply can't return there for another job."

Without any hesitation, he offered, "I'll accommodate your schedule and pay all of your expenses to travel back and forth at whatever frequency you want."

After discussing the offer with David and having several subsequent conversations with John, I decided I'd give it a go and accepted his offer. Then I started second-guessing my decision. I called Clay, sharing my reservations about whether I could truly succeed in this endeavor. I had never been in the private sector and certainly never helped anyone start or grow a practice or expand a business.

Clay said, "Rebecca, you have a proven record of top performance. You've done it for a decade. Just take the skills and leadership you've learned and applied in government and apply it to consulting. It isn't going to require any different skills than you have now. That and your hard work will translate into success."

I now had the confidence to bulldoze it forward with all I had. The learning once again began in a whole new area—one-on-one consulting. On April 4, 2005, I walked into the new opportunity in DC to reinvent myself in the private sector. It was the start of my crazy 1,500-mile commute back and forth between there and Austin that has continued for sixteen years at the writing of this book.

John became the CEO of that firm. He took me under his wing and taught me everything about the consulting world from soup to nuts. He knew the ins and outs of how to start and grow a business; it wasn't his first rodeo. With a great network and knack for attracting good people to work for him and a strong background in corporate HR, John had started several businesses but never worked in the federal government. That was a whole different beast. So, while he taught me about starting a business and the intricacies of the consulting world, I taught him about the federal human capital landscape. With his knowledge, my network, and our combined experiences, we made a great "tag team" for building his company's federal practice from scratch.

It only took about four months for me to cut my teeth in consulting and begin to see how very much I enjoyed it. In fact, it turned out I was really good at it. Within six months, I got the company our first client and federal contract.

For the first two years after returning to Texas, I traveled back and forth between Austin and DC every two weeks. It was a tremendous time of continued growth, stress, and stretching. At the same time, it was exciting. I thrived on learning and navigating the DC world of consulting. When there, I pulled long hours and frequently crammed a full fifty-hour work week into four days so that I could leave on Thursday evenings to be home Friday, Saturday, and Sunday with the family. To say I learned how to be a high-capacity mom, wife, executive, consultant, marketer, and networker would be an understatement.

All of my efforts paid off. Eventually, my federal practice earned well over 80 percent of the company's revenue. We experienced tremendous growth together. Within six years, the company's footprint had grown to more than ten agencies and $7 million in revenue, most of which came from the federal market.

CALLED BY POTUS TO SERVE AGAIN

When I left the White House job, I recommended a brilliant young man named Dr. Eric Motley as my replacement. He had graduated high school at age sixteen, earned his PhD at twenty-one, and came highly recommended to the administration by a former high-ranking official. All that in and of itself was impressive, but I fell in love with Eric's passion for life when I first met him in February 2001. Like me, he had been raised by his grandmother in poverty but achieved success nonetheless. He also has an amazing biography, *Madison Park: A Place of Hope*, about his tremendous journey. As he has spent most of his life in school expanding his education, he had never had a real full-time "career" job, but I was determined to train him in his first one—as one of my deputy directors in White House personnel.

Eric turned out to be one of my best hires and became highly successful in his life and career. When I left the White House and went off to U.S. Treasury, the director of White House Personnel accepted my recommendation to have Eric serve in my role with no reservation. Today, he serves as the executive vice president of the Aspen Institute in Washington DC. I was immensely proud of Eric and all he had achieved.

Late summer 2005, about six months after I left the administration, Eric called me. "Rebecca, first, how are you, David, and the kids doing? And how is your move to Texas and resettling?"

After I gave him a brief overview, he said, "Well, let me tell you the reason I'm calling. I was in the Oval Office with POTUS today, and your name came up. I was recommending a list of people who might serve on West Point Military Academy's board. When he saw your name as a potential, he immediately said, 'Ask Rebecca if she wants to serve on West Point.' So that brings me to the second reason why I'm calling you—POTUS would like to know if you'd like to serve as a member on West Point's board for a three-year term."

Honest to God, my jaw dropped, and I nearly fell over with shock. I finally managed to ask, "Eric, what about me and West Point makes sense? I don't have a military background. How am I a fit?"

His response brought both joy and tears to my eyes. "Well, my dear, POTUS said, 'Let's put Rebecca on that board. She'll know what to do and go shake that organization up with her management experience.'"

Once again, if POTUS felt I could do it, well, I was honored to accept the invitation. POTUS had only four appointments to make for that board. I knew that only one position was vacant, and the president was asking me to serve! It blew my mind!

After our call ended, I reminded myself that I did know the board well from overseeing it when I served in the White House and Eric had worked for me. I had also made prior recommendations to POTUS for the Academy and personally knew how some of the best and brightest in our country coveted those rare appointments. I could do this! I was up for the challenge, energized, and determined to represent POTUS on the board to the best of my talent and ability.

In September 2005, I received my commission to serve as a member on West Point Military Academy's board as one of five presidential appointees. One of the benefits was that it was a volunteer position, part-time, and met only three to four times a year. I could continue working in the consulting practice without it interfering with my day-to-day work. Of course, I was also tickled pink to serve and support President Bush in his second term. It was such a critical time in our nation because the entire view of training soldiers for war had dramatically changed. I would have a chance to help shape the future of one of the most important assets in our country—the young men and women who would graduate from West Point and serve in our military forces. Words can't describe the awe I felt.

Those three years were life-altering in many ways. My favorite part was the beginning of the campus year. The board was allowed to have lunch in the mess hall with the young men and women entering the Academy and listen to their stories of how they got there and why they wanted to serve their country in the Army.

In addition, on certain visits, I got to bring my husband and son to the campus. One summer when David and I brought Caleb, the superintendent arranged for him to sit in the cockpit of a Black Hawk helicopter. It was a wonderful and unique experience for all of us.

TIME TO INVEST IN LIVES

In the fall of 2005, my whole family was called to serve, and this time it was David's seventeen-year-old niece, Elicia. She was having challenges with her home life and had an altercation with her mother, David's younger sister, a single mom struggling with alcoholism at that time. A local judge ordered that Elicia could not live at home with her mother. Furthermore, tensions were high with her mom and Elicia was emotionally distraught, having a hard time in school, hanging out with the wrong crowd, and making poor choices.

David felt strongly that she was our priority. He said, "If we have a passion and vision to serve other kids in trouble in the inner city, then we need to start first with Elicia and invest in her, try to help her get on track in her school and with her life. I'm concerned she's failing and has no chance unless we intervene."

David and I prayed and talked with our son Caleb, who was in fifth grade. This was a family decision because it would affect him too. Crystaline was in a leadership training program in Dallas.

Convincing her mom that Elicia's visit to our home would actually be a long-term beneficial move was difficult because she loved her daughter. She didn't want her gone longer than a few weeks and didn't understand why things had to be the way they were. After many conversations, tears, and prayers, she agreed.

Elicia was eager because she and her uncle David were quite close, and she would be with her cousin KK (her nickname for Caleb). Elicia knew our stories and that we had come out of the same situation and succeeded, and she wanted a new life. We surrounded her with lots of love, support, structure, and discipline to help her get on track.

Once again, my hero, David, the family rock, stepped up to the plate and cared for both Caleb and Elicia while I continued commuting back and forth to DC and building the consulting practice.

Eighteen months later, in the summer of 2007, Elicia graduated from high school. We took her on her first trip with our family to Disney World, and she was ecstatic. If you ask Elicia today about moving in with us, she'd say that being part of a family unit of love, nurturing, faith, and all-around support for her was a catalyst of change in her life.

Elicia is like my second daughter. She is in her early thirties, has a successful career in the staffing industry and a beautiful son named Arrion, our great-nephew. They are both part of the fabric of our immediate family, and we remain enormously proud of her! Through Elicia, we learned how to put our vision in action. She helped train us for what lay ahead.

Looking back, I can see the path that was prepared for us, but *we* had to prepare and plan for it. Everything, no matter how small it seemed at the time, was a step closer to our purpose. It was all a time of more learning, more training, and more equipping.

We had studied hard and worked even harder, but we couldn't see what was ahead and around the bend. We didn't know that soon, we would graduate from this phase of our lives and be catapulted to the next level of our journey—entrepreneurship!

CHAPTER SEVEN

BECOMING AN eNTREPRENEUR

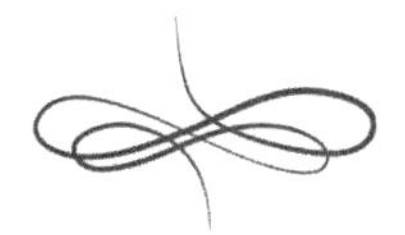

"The past is your lesson. The present is your gift. The future is your motivation."

— ZIG ZIGLAR

Everything was lining up, and we were ready to take another leap of faith. David had spent a few years with CONFIA, and it turned out to be a highly successful grassroots effort. At the same time, I was thriving in the consulting business and making good money. It made sense to bite the bullet now and go all in with our nonprofit by dedicating all of David's time to starting and building it from the ground up. That, of course, would mean he'd have to quit working a traditional paying job, and we'd have to become a one-salary household. His work with CONFIA had wrapped up and the timing was perfect.

We both were eager, David especially, particularly to help those boys growing up without fathers, something that resonated deeply within him given his own background. In the spring of 2008, our nonprofit, LaunchPad, was birthed with a vision and mission to serve inner-city kids. And we already had the perfect place to put it to good use—Dobie Middle School, located in one of the highest crime-ridden areas in our city.

It was all about timing. Maria, the dropout prevention specialist at Dobie, had heard about David's life story and accomplishments. Knowing he was an ideal fit to challenge and equip her students, she invited him to talk to a few of them.

She was a big advocate for these inner-city kids because she knew firsthand the struggles most of them faced both in the home and in an environment plagued by poverty and other negative socioeconomic factors. Maria herself grew up in poverty and, at a young age, watched her father shoot and kill her mother. Later in life, she got a job with the school district to try and keep students from dropping out of school. She was also a single mom living in the inner city, and two of her young kids were attending Dobie.

After meeting David and hearing him speak to her students, Maria supported our efforts to come onto Dobie's campus. It just so happened that seven of their male students had been caught skipping school, and the judge assigned them to a truancy class as an alternative to juvenile detention.

Maria told Ms. Chapman, the principal, about David and his LaunchPad program. Fortunately, Ms. Chapman was open to the idea. David started his first official after-school program with those boys, and as they say, the rest is history.

After we got to know Maria and she got to know us, David and I became mentors and advisors to her. I became interested in her story and saw an opportunity to help her work through her past trauma and change old thinking patterns that seemed to plague her from time to time.

Although she was employed at Dobie, she was a single mom in a lower income bracket that forced her to rely on government assistance. I encouraged her to get off the welfare system, but the drive to change and move forward came from her 100 percent. She was encouraged by my journey and wanted to learn everything she could about how to climb out of her situation and deal with her past.

During the few years I mentored her, she worked hard and got promoted in the school system and off government assistance. Her own children participated in the LaunchPad class while attending Dobie. When her daughter Christina moved on to high school, she became one of our group leaders for the LaunchPad girls.

Nearly ten years later, Maria and I remain good friends. She's an incredible woman who daily devotes her time, life, and passion to help inner-city youth and their families. She and her children were just a few of LaunchPad's first success stories, but they wouldn't be the last.

David continued to work hard at making a difference in the lives of these kids. His commitment started paying off in spades as we saw more success stories. Each transformed life reenforced that we were doing the right thing, and David was in a place where he could continue to invest in the lives of these young people and pursue his passion.

A NECESSARY SHIFT

The calendar had just turned the page to the year 2011. We were sitting in church one Sunday morning when suddenly the question hit me: *Why am I helping build someone else's company and wealth when I can build my own?*

I couldn't ignore it, nor could I come up with any good answer. It bothered me to know I was bringing in millions of dollars for John's firm, but at the end of the day, I was a W-2 employee. Granted, I had excelled and was making an incredible salary, but I wasn't an owner. Therefore, I couldn't share in any of the profits of ownership even though I had helped grow the firm's bottom line by nearly $6 million.

After we got home from church that morning, David and I discussed the idea (and dream) of starting my own consulting firm. I loved his outside-the-box thinking. He was a big encouragement to me, especially since I'm usually the calculated one with the reality check on the data and numbers.

However, in this new dream, the numbers didn't add up. I knew it was risky leaving my high-paying job of over $200,000 a year, a solid 401(k) plan, and health insurance for our entire family. Just a few years earlier, David had left a senior-level manager's salary to become a nonprofit social entrepreneur, and people don't work for nonprofits to make a lot of money, especially when it's your own. So, if I wasn't bringing home a salary, there would be no real, steady income.

Regardless, here I was contemplating starting my own company. Despite what appeared to be a lack of logic, I felt motivated, energized, and excited about the possibility, even if it meant beginning with nothing. But I didn't have nothing. I had a network in DC. If I could help someone else start their federal practice from the ground up, why couldn't I do it for myself?

I again sought counsel from Clay and others I knew who had started a business. My older brother Daniel was in year four or five of starting a business with his wife. Daniel had also left a high-paying job to start over, and I was encouraged by his story. If he could do it, why not me?

Oftentimes, to achieve great things, we must take giant leaps and strides that seem crazy on the surface. It could mean going backwards, particularly financially, for a time to pursue and follow our dreams. It involves sacrifice on some level. David and I prepared as much as we could. We would save as much as possible for a "cushion" and cut our expenses to the bare minimum until I won our first contract.

I took time in my next DC trip to talk with a few folks on the ground who I trusted and who knew the DC consulting world, current and former government colleagues and now friends. Everywhere I turned for counsel, all I heard was, "You should do it. You'll be very successful. I know it."

There was one person in particular I wanted to reach out to, an IT developer named Bill. I had met him in early 2007 through a friend in my church community. Bill needed help navigating the second term of the Bush White House. He was facing a challenge with a government contract he had with one of the agencies, and he thought perhaps someone who had worked for the White House could provide him counsel. At that time, Bill was a small business owner of an IT firm in DC. Back in the Clinton days and into the early Bush days, he made millions of dollars building one of the largest web-based procurement portals for the federal government (now called FedBiz Ops).

I reached out to Bill in the spring of 2011, and I learned he had started to wind down his IT firm. I told him about my plans to start my own consulting company. I shared with him that the only obstacle to leaving my current job was leaving behind a large steady salary. I explained that David had already left his full-time job to start and run our nonprofit. One of us had to bring in a minimum amount of income to pay our bills.

He listened intently and asked a few questions here and there. Then he said, "If you do this, I'll be your partner and give you the money to help you live for the first year until we win our own work. You can pay me back later with no interest after you make money, but no rush. Take your time. We would make a good team."

Wow! Just an amazing affirmation that this was what I needed to do.

We discussed more details. He suggested we start a company that complemented both of our backgrounds. We agreed to build a combined HR-IT firm that would provide a one-stop shop to the federal government. Since his other IT firm might conflict with his full-time work for our company, I asked if he would be willing to shut it down and focus his efforts on helping me start our business. He agreed to do so.

His interest and offer to help financially were the final pieces to the puzzle; however, David didn't know him. I wanted to make sure David met him and was fully on board. Throughout our marriage, we had always made every major decision together, and this certainly qualified as a major decision.

So that spring, David flew to DC to meet Bill and his wife, and we talked about the plan over dinner in their home. Then David and I talked about it on the way back to Texas. Once he gave his blessing and full support, I felt 100 percent charged.

However, it still wasn't a done deal. We had not yet finalized how we would structure the ownership operating agreement. Bill wanted equal decision-making, and I had planned to get my 8(a) Program Minority Owned Small Business Certification from the Small Business Administration (SBA), a powerful tool that gives the company flexibility for what the government refers to as "limited competitive contracts." The operating agreement was one piece of proof required to qualify for the minority certification as a business owned by a Hispanic-American individual who's presumed socially and economically disadvantaged. Per SBA regulations, the day-to-day governing and decision-making had to rest 100 percent on the certified individual—in this case, me. SBA required me to have majority ownership (51 percent control) with true majority decision-making on all things financial, all things staffing, and all things strategy and operations. After a lengthy discussion with Bill where I demonstrated the value to our company this certification would bring, he agreed that I should have 51 percent ownership, making me the majority owner.

Our roles were outlined. I would be the CEO and the "face" for marketing and branding. He would serve as minority owner and provide critical back-end office support, insights and experience in running a business, and expertise in the IT arena—something we wanted to distinctly include in the new firm's capabilities. We agreed to collaborate on ideas and work toward common goals. Overall, we knew the partnership would benefit both of us.

We decided to focus consulting services around four core capabilities, or what we called service offerings to the government: human capital (HR), organizational development (OD), business operations (BO), and information technology (IT). We would be a one-stop shop for the needs of organizations.

Shortly after laying out the details of our practice with Bill, I approached John, my current employer, where I was serving as executive vice president. I thanked him for allowing me to serve in his business and for supporting me in my overall success. Then I told him I planned to submit my resignation and asked if he would let me out of my noncompete agreement. This is usually in place with private sector firms to prevent successful employees from starting their own company in the exact same area and competing with their past employer.

About a week later, John came back to me and said, "Rebecca, after all you've done for this company, I plan to let you out of your noncompete. You're going to do amazing on your own, and I wouldn't want to keep you from that."

I later learned that he was able to do this because he held majority decision-making in his company. This incident confirmed my reasons for structuring our company with 51 percent ownership for myself. I am a bottom-line manager and have a very distinct way I like to set the tone and run an organization; therefore, majority ownership was ideal.

I gave John my word that in AG's first year, I would not solicit his clients or take his employees. We shook on it. I submitted my resignation and moved on. Thankfully, it worked out well, especially because things at that firm, which were out of my control, had started to unravel.

On April 11, 2011, I was off to start my own consulting business. Exactly one month later, AvantGarde LLC (AG) was born with only my partner, Bill, and me.

I hit the pavement to market AG across the federal government within my network and beyond but kept my word to John. I left his clients and employees alone for that entire first year, and I did not directly solicit them. It is incredible, however, that as soon as I alerted clients to my departure, they began sending me text messages and calling to say, "We're happy for you, but where you go, we go." On their own, two of our former clients reached out to AG and began to engage us. As the government can work with whomever they want, I left the issue alone and thanked God I had earned that reputation of trust long term.

In that second year as we started to grow, I also began to get calls from my former team members at the previous firm who wanted to join AG. They expressed their desire to continue to work with me and applied on their own for open positions within the company. Several of those long-term team members who joined in that first year and two of AG's original staff are still with me today.

The irony in the timing of all of this was that shortly after I resigned, I learned that John had planned to get out of his firm as well, so my advocate and champion would have been leaving anyway. He would have then handed the company over his partner who would become the new CEO. We weren't compatible in our style of governing or leading, so it really was best in the long term.

The God-timing, as I like to call it, could not have been more perfect.

FIRST REVENUE OUT OF THE GATE

My first client was the U.S. Department of Agriculture (USDA) with a small contract of about $50,000. Getting an award of this size in month six of having your doors open with no prior vendor performance was a tremendous accomplishment! I was grateful for that USDA client's trust, something I had evidently earned years earlier when we had worked together in my prior federal life.

The second contract came six months later, at the end of our first year, with the Department of Justice (DOJ). It was the result of an incredible amount of hard work and a strong networking relationship I had with a prior manager in US Treasury back in 2004. He had taken a new job at DOJ and was experiencing tremendous challenges implementing an IT system for a large project. He knew my reputation for managing change on a grand scale and producing results, and Bill's past IT performance was the icing on the cake.

When this project came to my attention, however, I knew that AG's small size and short tenure as a business wouldn't be able to win that contract. Our competitors were large consulting firms with hundreds of millions (in some cases, billions) in revenue and tremendous experience implementing large IT systems across the entire federal government, both of which AG lacked. So, I decided to find a way to collaborate with a larger company and secure my first vendor relationship to help me grow. After knocking on many doors without any success, I utilized my network to find the right company.

DOJ was going to release the bid for the contract under a particular procurement schedule that about twenty large companies owned. Procurement schedule awards are often competing and given to a select group of companies that can do what the government calls "streamlined bidding" when new work is needed. I found someone who knew the vice president of a large IT firm with a decades-long record of strong contract support to DOJ. I made a cold call to this VP, introduced myself, and told her about my prior background in the Bush administration as well as my new company. She agreed to meet with me in person to gauge interest and discuss the potential for collaboration.

We immediately hit it off and discovered we had a ton in common in terms of our approach to serving the government and our strategy in how effective large-scale initiatives were executed. We even had some federal relationships in common with other agency executives. Because I had a relationship with the DOJ prospect and common ideas about how we could make an impact, I convinced her I had agency insights that would give us a competitive edge. I committed to do my best to not only bring the right team to the table, but also to be a great long-term strategic subcontract partner.

She liked what I had to say. It so happened that she and I also shared the same expertise as human capital organizational change agents. Together with a smart team, we crafted a winning proposal and approach that led to our selection for the award—a big one with over $11 million in revenue over five years.

Before the proposal bid went to the agency, I also negotiated that AG would receive 30 percent of the contract value if we won it as a team. Negotiating revenue work share is a key strategy to ensuring that any vendor-teaming relationship results in a win that produces actual revenue. Securing a work share commitment up front allowed AG to hire our own IT staff. This represented nearly $4 million just for AG.

Consequently, Bill and I got to hire several of the people assigned to the first AG strategic partner's contract serving DOJ. Bill had worked with the IT team that we assigned to this project when he had his prior company, so he knew they did a good job, and they trusted him. They were a great fit for his current team, so we put them on the AG payroll.

That was the start of a flow of new work that we are performing to this day. We hired our first four employees that fall and were on our way with AG!

It's hard to describe the feeling of being an employer and having the ability to put people to work and give them opportunities to grow in their careers. This is probably the most important part of my work at AG, knowing that we are supporting employee growth and development. Many people did it for me early on when I was in a place of little options. As I grew in my career, my cheerleaders remained behind me, supporting me.

Now I'm paying it forward. Knowing that the futures of these employees are in my hands gives me an awesome feeling of humility. I do everything I can to make sure I continue to give people jobs and support their advancement so that they can succeed. My partner Bill shares that value and having a common goal has served us well.

SOCIAL ENTREPRENEUR IMPACT AS LAUNCHPAD ALSO GROWS!

By late fall of 2011, it had been a little over three years since LaunchPad started serving kids in the inner city and providing daily teaching of core values and leadership after school. Ms. Chapman was still the campus principal. She started to notice the impact David's class was making on a small select group of students who were rising up to demonstrate leadership on campus. She came to David and asked him what he needed in order to expand his program across the entire campus and simultaneously teach numerous classes.

David's answer was simple—resources to hire manpower. She quickly mobilized to spearhead a grant from the Texas Education Agency targeted for after-school programming to serve 130 kids a week. Then she recommended David and his LaunchPad team to be the primary recipient of the grant.

Without reservation, David accepted the challenge and geared up! That year, he hired the team, created the curriculum, and launched the program campus-wide. In a matter of weeks, David had gone from being a one-man instructor to hiring a full-time program coordinator and securing ten other vendor subs to come to the campus and teach their programs, everything from chess club to arts and crafts, STEM (Science, Technology, Engineering, and Math), film, music, and other areas.

A few months into the first year of that grant, David and his team were serving hundreds of inner-city kids through the after-school program. For the first time since David and I met back in 1988, we felt like we had come full circle, returning to our roots.

LaunchPad was getting tremendous traction in the city, and we saw real lives and behaviors changed through David and his team. They created a sustainable impact and transformation for that school campus community. We saw wonderful metrics and outcomes, such as increased school attendance, a downtick in truancy cases referred to a judge, improved grades, and behaviors that aligned with the core values curriculum that David taught, such as leadership, trust, respect, positive choices, and the power of education, to name a few.

As we grew, David was deliberate in developing partnerships with the University of Texas at Austin, the Greater Austin Hispanic Chamber of Commerce, the Austin

Police Department, and local businesses, including a Hispanic franchise owner of several McDonald's and others interested in investing in LaunchPad.

Even in the midst of starting and growing AG, I played a heavy role in LaunchPad's administrative management and provided support to David and its fundraising aspects. When I was in town, I would volunteer on the campus to be a small part of what was happening there as well as taking on coaching and ad hoc teaching for some of the young girls enrolled in his program. Together, we spent many long nights and days preparing for large-scale events for the students and parents at the school, such as David's annual HOMBRE, a community festival that drew a thousand fathers, sons, and male caretakers for a day of team building and unity. The event was focused on advocating the value of a father or male mentor in these young people's lives. The chief of police with APD even came out to speak to the groups and support our community events. Watching David work with those kids, those "diamonds in the rough" as he called them, was a phenomenal sight. His passion to roll up his sleeves and serve them and their families was second to none.

As cofounders, we made a great team, but this was tested many times. We're quite opposite in many respects. We share similar passions, but our methods of operating are different. He's a visionary and tends to see the bigger picture whereas I'm a manager and have an administration brain and like tactical action planning. Consequently, we tended to butt heads. At the same time, we learned to play to each other's strengths over the years and not force a square peg into a round hole.

So, David handled the front end as the visionary, "boots on the ground," and face of LaunchPad. I volunteered my time and took care of the back end and its administrative functions, such as onboarding and offboarding LaunchPad vendors, paying them, organizing QuickBooks for the nonprofit—you name it, I did it. Together, we raised money and marketed our work and LaunchPad's cause.

We made it happen. Over the course of a decade, the LaunchPad program served more than 3,000 inner-city kids and their families and received numerous awards and accolades. It became known as one of the top-performing after-school programs in the Austin school district.

Those ten years were the most intense in terms of stress and scheduling demands, but they were also the most rewarding and a time of growth once again for our marriage and family. The satisfaction and deep-down, eternal rewards when you pay it forward and invest in lives are amazing.

David never gave up on those kids. Today, some of our LaunchPad graduates have attended college, gotten their degrees, earned certifications in chef school and beauty school, served in the Armed Forces—you name it. We are extremely proud to have had a small part in their journey to success.

Another plus that came out of our LaunchPad years was our son-in-law, Chris. We had hired him as our campus project coordinator, and three years later he got engaged to and married our daughter, Crystaline.

In 2017, after numerous shifts in campus leadership, we decided not to reapply for a new grant. Instead, we have transitioned LaunchPad to funding various special projects and nonprofits with a focus on several key areas with which we resonate: youth empowerment and education, single mothers, teen pregnancy outreach, inner-city and community impact, and special programs driven by the community's need. For example, in 2020, during one of the biggest crises in America—the COVID-19 pandemic—we partnered with another local nonprofit and small business to feed over 3,000 nurses and doctors working long shifts and practically sequestered in their hospital. We were just so glad we could help. David and I firmly believe that supporting special philanthropic causes is an important fabric in our marriage and life.

AG EXPLODES

In the meantime, AG in DC was exploding. In its second year, we experienced over 700 percent growth. Just incredible! In years three through six, we continued to see 49 to 75 percent growth each year. In year eleven, we're still experiencing double-digit percentage growth annually and have about 110 employees spread across six states. Sometimes, I pinch myself and wonder has this really happened?

Each time I look back, I can see more of the details and steps of my entire life's amazing journey of transformation, of milestones, of change, and of reinventing myself, so that by the time I had hit this phase, it was seamless. I flowed right into it as if it was the most natural thing in the world.

From the outside looking in, however, it can appear crazy—around 500 trips on a plane over the past fifteen years; all of those long days of "hitting the DC grind," as we call it; all of those long hours spent in airports; and all of the time spent on Zoom calls and teleconferences at home. I've run a company virtually, led teams and grew the business even when I couldn't be in DC.

Looking back, looking at the present, and gazing into the future, all in all things worked out better than beautifully! For two drug-addicted kids with significant emotional and physical trauma issues, both limited in their formal education, one of them from the hood, living in poverty with little options, we had audacious faith, an unstoppable work ethic, and made life work for us. We seized the moments and soared.

We're proof that regardless of which side of the tracks you were born and raised on, regardless of the cards life dealt you, you are the one who decides your path, and the sky is the limit for what you can achieve.

I know it's not easy, especially with a past of bad mistakes. As the main character of author Susan Elizabeth Phillip's novel *Heaven, Texas* declares, "Anything worth having is worth fighting for." And fight we have because our faith, our present, our future, our family, our careers, our purpose are all worth it. Through it all, we remained faithful, and God allowed us to experience His miracles along the way. For sure, it's been an incredible journey, but for sure, it's not over.

Now when I close my eyes at night, the nightmares are gone and replaced by sound sleep. I rest knowing my life is on track and impactful, and that everything I dream is possible. Never, never stop dreaming, planning, hoping, and working hard.

ePILOGUE

It's not easy to make big transitions, and that includes totally reinventing yourself to become a business entrepreneur. Although the thought of being a small business owner and getting behind the wheel of my own career and destiny invigorated me, it also scared me quite a bit.

I had always worked for someone else—fifteen years in government and then six years for John when I began my consulting career. As an employee, I had a safety net of an employer, health insurance, and a 401(k). Every two weeks, my paycheck hit our bank account in the form of an automatic deposit. I could count on it as well as the amount—executive-level earnings and a great end-of-year bonus compensation package. Additionally, missteps in management didn't come out of my pocket nor did it change how others outside the company viewed me. My employer absorbed the costs and the disgruntled client's backlash.

As a business owner, all the decisions and all the rewards and consequences fall on me. The safety net is gone. Many times, I have no control over how much I get paid, and if things go bad, I actually lose money. I hate to lose anything. Plus,

I can work hard and invest hundreds or thousands of dollars to submit the best proposal, but someone else can come in and take that account away from AG.

In 2020, for example, we lost two major long-term clients representing millions of dollars in revenue after years of hard work and exceptional service to them, all simply due to the competitive nature of our business and what the government calls the "lowest price technically acceptable (LPTA) contractor selection process." That's lost money, literally gone in days, but in business, that's the risk you take. You go in there knowing you're going to win some and you're going to lose some. And hopefully, if you have a reputable, strong business, as we have built with AG, you win more than you lose.

It's also life. Life comes with ups and downs. Sometimes you excel, and other times you fail; it's inevitable. How you navigate that failure is key. I have learned over the years to fall forward and not allow it to drag me down. Often, when I ran across tough issues or faced obstacles that could lead to failure, Clay would say, "Rebecca, it sounds like an opportunity for you to excel." I learned how to navigate complexity, challenges, and yes, even failure.

Due to my realist nature, it was easy to allow myself to see only the negative and let fears and doubts stop me. Throughout my AG journey, I tried hard to focus on the positive instead of the negative, knowing the good that would come from owning a business—building a team and providing jobs and careers to people. In the end, the positive outweighed the negative, and I'm so glad! This doesn't mean I don't get sad or angry when loss happens; it just means I learn to work through those feelings and move past those emotions and try to encourage people, particularly in my management oversight, to continue forward. I believe good things happen to those who endure and often wait. Those losses we sustained in 2020 were significant, but the wins we sustained in the first and second quarters of 2021 far exceeded the losses. We will close out 2021 with continued financial growth and success!

Owning a small business provides intangible benefits, too. It has allowed me to be the captain of my own ship, and the sky is the limit! I can stretch as far as I want, and at the end of the day, I get compensated with the money I earned from my hard work.

Having our own money has enabled David and me to support our family and philanthropic causes like LaunchPad and others (a major core value for us), realize our dreams of travel and other experiences, and when it's time, secure our retirement. We knew early on, the only way to build that legacy of wealth and impact was to be an entrepreneur and build a business. The power that brings can be extremely rewarding. Women-owned small businesses are the fastest-growing demographic in America! I am proud and honored to be in that group.

When I worked in the White House for Bush's first term, I didn't realize just how important the small business market was and is to the fabric of our nation, but President Bush did. My husband, David, worked at SBA in those first two years of the administration, and he supported their mission and knew their value. From early on, President Bush placed a major focus on small businesses and said that they are the engine of America; they are what make our economy go. Now that I'm a small business owner and contribute to the U.S. economy, I can see just how right he was!

Being a small business owner allows me to set the mission and vision that are important to me and then pass my values into, throughout, and beyond my company. Business ownership has allowed me to venture into territories not yet seen or experienced in my career. In 2015, my AG partner, Bill, and I applied for a patent for our own software platform. Six years later in the spring of 2021, we were finally issued our official patent—a tremendous accomplishment. Bill and I became co-patent owners of an agile web-based methodology called the Workforce Management Office tool (WMO) that aligns a client's workforce to their business needs.

WMO offers multi-faceted, integrated, and predictive data analysis. When combined with the expert AG consulting team, senior managers are given the information and guidance they need to make informed data-driven decisions in all major areas of strategic human capital, organizational design, and workforce and mission alignment.

WMO's capability has been a distinct differentiator for AG. I believe its proprietary platform is unique in the market. Being able to say "I own a patent" and offering services as a software provider are thrilling!

WMO started as a brilliant concept Bill had early in our firm's development, and years later, we are realizing the results! That's what America is all about—the land of opportunity and possibility!

OUR CORE AT AG

From the beginning, I wanted the core of AG's values system to be loving and treasuring our number-one asset—our people. This book is certainly not intended to be a self-help entrepreneur book. But since you're here at this point, I thought it would be helpful to share some secrets to our AG success.

First, hands down, our best strategy is recruiting and retaining good people. Second is to allow them to thrive in their expertise and use their talents to the best of their abilities. I have always had a knack for attracting talented project managers, smart experts, and high-performing teams. From day one as CEO, I placed this strategy at the forefront of everything at the firm, so the AG management team aligns with our core values.

I'm a strong believer that any CEO is only as good as their team. Period. In chapter 7, I said that good people can make or break you. That's a definite when you're a CEO. In my view, a CEO with a good strategy but an inability to keep good people is a recipe for failure. But a CEO with a good strategy *and great* people—now that's a recipe for success, and as Clay would say, "Great results and outcomes are what management is all about."

In January 2021, I decided to launch our first AG climate culture survey to check the pulse of our 110-plus workforce across six dimensions including leadership, culture/climate, employee satisfaction, company benefits, communication, and work-life balance. To my surprise, we had nearly 90 percent of employees participate with an average score of 92-97 percent positive ratings across these indicators. It was mind-blowing feedback, confirming that we are on the right track, doing the right things to serve and support our core team. It was a major testament to how hard our management team has worked to implement our core values all the way down to each employee they serve.

We have also made a point to ensure that every AG employee is heard, and their opinion is valued. Sure, we have our standard hiccups like most small businesses, but they pale in comparison to the success our team has achieved and the experiences of collaboration and engagement they bring to work every day. I'm immensely proud of both our management and AG team—they are some of the smartest people I have had the pleasure to lead—and how they support all of our clients throughout AG and help us achieve success.

It's a two-way street, though. We have a great history of promoting employees to give them opportunities to grow in their career at AG. As we grow as a company and take on new clients and contracts, in turn, they grow with us in their own personal journey and career. Their success is my success.

AG'S "WITH YOU, NOT TO YOU" APPROACH

We also value our clients, but until they work with us to experience it, we're just another vendor, and vendors are a dime a dozen in the federal government. As I mentioned earlier, just when you think you've secured a lifetime client, another vendor can come in with the lowest bid and take your work away from you. So, we've established differentiators to make us stand out from the rest.

One of our differentiators we use in all of our consulting engagements, also a second secret to AG's success, is what Clay taught me nearly twenty years ago—the "with you, not to you" approach. We listen, learn, and execute not what we think the clients need but what they tell us they need in a method that is collaborative, engaging, and power packed.

When decision makers are trying to choose between us and other vendors, I want them to understand the unique value we bring to the table. I'll explain, "We're only the right firm if you allow us to employ our 'with you, not to you' approach. This means we need you collaboratively working with us and valuing our team's ability and expertise to execute your mission."

We don't assume to be the smartest consulting firm on the block. We just want to be known as the uniquely collaborative and engaging firm with smart, talented people who achieve our clients' goals.

It's an approach clients seem to appreciate.

We also provide another differentiator, which is our ability to move from a vendor to a trusted advisor role within the first six months of a contract. I tell our team, "If a client likes you, that's great. But in order to sustain that client, they have to trust you and us. Trust takes time to build."

When clients learn to trust you and things go wrong (as they do), regardless of who's at fault, it's much easier to have a transparent conversation about what happened and the lessons learned so it can be prevented in the future. They'll also share details with you about what's coming down the pipeline—new needs and organizational and people issues they're grappling with—and engage you in helping them solve the problems.

Undoubtedly, government has problems just like any major organization. We want to be known as solution-oriented and the go-to firm that helps solve these problems. That doesn't happen with a check-the-box vendor. It only works with a trusted advisor. Our AG team works to build that trust. Once we gain it, it goes a long way to sustain that client, sometimes even beyond the competitive process.

There are many other strategies and secrets to AG's success, too many to divulge in an epilogue. Perhaps one day, I will bare them in a book geared solely for entrepreneurs.

DREAM BIG

Becoming an entrepreneur and small business owner has been exciting, challenging, stretching (more than any other stretching I have ever undertaken), and exhausting. But oh, has it been worth it! I can't encourage you enough to set your goals, plan, work hard, and dream big. It is the formula for success. Never, never give up on your dreams, even when the odds and obstacles seem stacked against you and even when the noise around you seems deafening and negative voices are dragging you down.

We live in a country with tremendous opportunity for those who work hard, prepare and plan, do their best to do right by people, and "play well in the sandbox." It's how many of my successful friends, who started their lives with little to offer, overcame tremendous odds and hardships.

We've all been given a talent, but as President John F. Kennedy said, "All of us do not have equal talent, but all of us should have an equal opportunity to develop our talents." Your talent is no less important than mine and vice versa. It's our unique abilities that make up this world. We all must do our part to contribute as well as help each other to succeed.

Develop the talent you've been entrusted with and cultivate the skill that can emerge from it. When I've done this, unfathomable opportunities have opened up. And they're just waiting for you to grab hold of them too!

Again, dream big! *IT IS POSSIBLE!*

AUTHOR'S REFLECTIONS

You may be surprised to learn that the initial concept for *Lost Girl* was a self-help book. But when I started writing the details of my story, I realized that giving snippets of it would not adequately convey the powerful transformation and amazing journey I have experienced in my life. You need to know everything in-between to see and appreciate the whole picture. As I started telling the story, I began to see the common themes that every person is faced with—themes of loss, tragedy, bad choices, unforeseen hurts, toxic relationships, and the peaks and the valleys of life. Therefore, *Lost Girl* is a story that nearly everyone can see themselves in and through.

Although this is a memoir, I would be remiss if I didn't leave you with some of my thoughts and tips that have served as essential action steps for reengineering the various parts of my thought processes, heart condition, attitudes, and mindsets, all necessary for my growth.

In these last few pages, I want to leave you with five core drivers that have served as the fuel to keep me pushing forward through thick and thin, as well as some takeaways to serve as food for thought in your own journey through life, family, career, and faith.

FIVE CORE DRIVERS IN MY LIFE

1) Faith

My faith in God has served as a core foundation in my life. There is no way I could have escaped from the destruction that awaited me if I had not taken the action steps necessary to change and experienced God's miracles along the way. He has demonstrated His love for me and His faithfulness again and again. Consequently, I've learned that when everything seems to be unraveling, God is there, guiding me, encouraging me, and giving me favor and fuel for my journey.

However, I'm not naïve when it comes to faith. Having faith alone is not sufficient. God does His part, but when He bestows favor, when He blesses us with a miracle, when He opens a door of opportunity, when He heals us, then we must do our part, even when it's hard work, and often uncomfortable or even painful. Things don't just suddenly change or course-correct without putting in the necessary effort on our part.

For example, my mother's faith in Jesus was one of the strongest I've known, yet she never followed up and took the necessary steps to deal with her issues, trauma, and past hurts; she suppressed them. Therefore, when she got cancer, she didn't have the foundation that should have been part of her own transformation. Sadly, she died prematurely because of severe depression and loss of value in herself. She lost her fight to live. During the last ninety days of her life, I remember hearing her doctor declare, "Grace, you've lost the will to fight. In order to beat this cancer, you must have the will to live and fight." He was right. In the end, she gave up hope. She struggled with mental illness and depression, and in that last year, she never came out of it. In essence, depression took my mom, not cancer.

Hope and faith go hand in hand. Hebrews 11:1 (AMP) tells us, "Now faith is the assurance (title deed and confirmation) of things hoped for (divinely guaranteed), and the evidence of things not seen [the conviction of their reality—faith comprehends as fact what cannot be experienced by the physical sense]."

My experience with God instills great hope, and that hope gives me faith in His transformative power, and faith that He has a bigger plan for me, even though I may not see it. Regardless, I speak positivity and possibility into the atmosphere even when I don't always see it. I stand on my faith and not my fear in every single situation life brings my way. Meditation, prayer, and the study of God's Word give me the necessary tools as I relentlessly pursue God's purpose for my life.

2) Capacity

As our desire to change increases, so does our capacity to handle it. We must not let our current capabilities or limitations determine our ability to transform or cause us to doubt our ability to increase. Just like a runner, we must push beyond what we believe is our breaking point, and when we do, we find that our capacity has grown. You'll never know how much you can take and where you can actually go without taking the necessary steps to stretch or try.

I've been put in situations where I've had no choice but to increase my capacity, whether I initially thought I could (or wanted to) or not. I have frequently been thrown into new roles or foreign tasks that I'm not familiar with and certainly not comfortable doing. But I've pushed through, and my capacity to learn, to change, to love, to multitask, to do anything—all improved.

A great example in my life was my capacity to learn. I was a terrible student in school. I was told I wasn't smart enough and believed that I was a failure. But once my spiritual metamorphosis started and I got my first real job, the transformation began to take place in my mind, in my belief system, and in my attitude about hard work. My motivation to get my daughter and me off welfare caused me to become a sponge and soak up everything, learning what I could to make up for what I didn't know. My confidence increased upon realizing I could build my capacity for knowledge, and I went for it. I studied hard, leveraged lessons from mentors, and applied my new expertise to try things I had never done before. As a result, I slowly increased my ability to take on more. When I didn't know the answer to something or how to do it, I figured it out.

Thirty years later, I'm running an $18 million company, editing policy documents, and directly managing finances and people on a large scale. Along the way, I have established myself as an expert in my field. This is coming from a person who barely passed fundamentals in math in high school and made dismal grades in her sophomore and junior years before dropping out. If I can do it, so can you!

3) Hard Work

The drive to work hard is innate in some, but others have to develop a discipline for it. I belonged in the latter group. Working hard didn't come to me naturally. Like it or not, though, hard work is a requirement for success, even at the cost of changing old mindsets and habits that have been negatively impacting our bottom line. Lailah Gifty Akita summed it up quite well when she said, "Hard work is the formula for success."

Yes, it's hard work to deal with your past, your pain, your trauma, and your abuse. It's hard work to learn a new skill, to stay married thirty-one years, to be an entrepreneur. But in the end, if you persevere, you will reap the rewards. Understand, even with hard work, sometimes we fail and don't fully realize the intended outcomes we want to see in life. But ensuring we stay the course and consistent despite the current picture is essential to keep moving forward.

4) Mentors/Advisors

Don't do it alone. I didn't. Otherwise, my success would have been stunted, and I probably wouldn't have written this book you're reading now. My husband and family played a key role in my transformation, and my mentors and coaches helped me to look at things differently, to think and behave differently, and to reinvent myself. When we face challenges, we're more likely to be successful with a partner, mentor, friend, or confidant than if we go it alone. There is tremendous power in working together. Multiple ideas and viewpoints are always better than one.

My choice not to fly solo was *so* critical in my journey that I made sure I pointed out the impact of teamwork, collaboration, and mentoring in this book. I knew early on I needed to find people I looked up to who were successful and who I could emulate, who I could reach out to for guidance. Consequently, I ended up with those who believed in me, partnered with me, propelled me, and encouraged me through my professional career and life. People are more willing to help those who admit they need help and are teachable than those who are too timid to ask or prideful and think they already know it all.

To this day, I have a circle of people, both men and women, in my life who I bounce ideas off of. There is little I do in terms of big steps without first running it by my trusted friends and advisors. God never intended for us to do life alone; we need others and people in order to live life to the fullest. For me, it has been important ensuring that the "others" who are providing counsel and support have something to bring to the table. In turn, I offer similar value to them.

5) Vision

Finally, you must have a vision, an ability to see a mission, concept, or dream that has yet to take place, and plan accordingly all the way through to conception. This, along with passion, are two major components to help you grow, learn, and thrive. Without vision, dreams and goals are never achieved, and even worse, they will never even get off the ground and can die.

My husband and best friend, David, has taught me through example to have *big*, audacious visions. He is a natural-born visionary, a dreamer, but for me it was a learned skill over at least a decade. When we first married, I was unable to see past my own issues and obstacles. I'm the realist in our marriage and tend to evaluate things through a black and white lens. But once I learned how to join him in visioning, it became easier to dream and look past what didn't look so ideal to see the color in what had first appeared to be all black and white.

I am proof that where you start in life doesn't always have to be where you finish. When things are outside of our control (as they often are), I remain centered by faith and a strong emphasis on vision to see what is possible beyond the here and now. Learning to incorporate vision into your life is an essential part of expanding your world.

TOP TAKEAWAYS

The last thirty-plus years of my transformation journey have included so many gold nuggets that have helped me pivot quickly through the different shifts. The following are the top seven that can serve as takeaways from this book:

1) Understand your value and identity.

Some of us who grew up in dysfunction or encountered tragedy and abuse in life struggle to understand our true identity. We shape our view and actions based on our experiences and on the people who impacted us, good or bad.

For so many years, I thought I was a mistake, but then at the age of twenty, God told me differently. In Jeremiah 1:5 (NIV), He proclaims, "Before I formed you in the womb I knew you, before you were born I set you apart…."

I had to understand that what happened to me wasn't truly who I was but the result of circumstances created by the bad environment I grew up in or my poor choices as a young teen. I accepted early on that I was simply a lost girl. But then I discovered that wasn't where I was to stay. Somewhere in the dark, God found me. He put a desire in me to pursue change, and He placed certain people in my life who had achieved success and could help me relearn and reshape myself into the woman He created me to be.

Understanding your value and identity is powerful. In his book *Identity Leadership*, New York Times best-selling author Stedman Graham gives some pointers to help us get there. Graham writes, "Who you are has to do with your talents, your abilities, your dreams, and your aspirations. It can sometimes take a lifetime to be comfortable in your own skin and uncover your true self. To find out your true self requires a person to dive down into your core level in order to release, sharpen and operate in your unique gifts and talents. Focus on your own journey to discover what motivates and energizes you to do the things you love to do with abilities only you possess."

Our past mistakes are not where we find our value and identity. Our actions from here on out give us opportunities to change both for the better.

2) Trauma breeds trauma. Deal with it, or it will deal with you!

My personal trauma existed through my childhood and teen years and carried into my adult life and early marriage, seeking to destroy me. When we don't deal with traumatic issues in our past or present, we risk seeing life—or worse, acting out our lives—through that lens of trauma. We've all seen the harmful effects from being hurt and how hurt people will hurt other people. I lived it with my mom. Digging out her past suffering was too painful, so she masked it with her faith and service in the church. But deep down inside, it manifested in the last ten years of her life in many destructive ways. I tried to help her get professional help or seek counseling. Her response was, "Why? It doesn't matter. I am who I am now." It was heartbreaking.

Getting past the hurt can be difficult. For me, it was about three core solutions:

1) **Face it head on**! Facing my trauma and traumatizers didn't always happen in person or face-to-face, but facing them in my heart, soul, mind, and spirit provided much-needed closure.
2) **Learn to deal with it**! It was crucial that I learned my trigger points and stayed committed to dealing with the trauma, not just once or twice when it surfaced, but until healing took place. Getting help, whether from a third-party counselor or confidant, gave me a more balanced perspective as well as a vocal acknowledgement.
3) **Learn to let go!** Moving past the pain and trauma required me to make the choice to forgive and let go of it. Once I did, I felt unexpectedly free! When you get to this point, never pick it back up, and when you feel like you want to go backwards, sit down and write a list of your achievements. Focus on the positive moves you have made. They will keep you from giving in to the negative urge to look back. Keep a journal of thankfulness where you can write down what you are thankful for. It's amazing what begins to happen in your mind and spirit when you display gratitude.

3) Forgiveness is the secret sauce.

Forgiving those who hurt, offend, betray, or abuse you is crucial. Forgiving yourself is equally powerful. I had to do both. It wasn't easy. People I trusted, including myself, who were supposed to care for and love me, did so many bad things to me, but I had to set my mind to forgive them. And I had to try and see their behavior through their lens.

In my life, forgiveness accomplished three goals:

1) Reset my lens toward those who hurt me as I sought to learn why.
2) Reset my self-worth so I wouldn't keep beating myself up internally.

3) Gave me the freedom to love my offenders where they were (again, including myself). Keep in mind that not everyone has the capacity to love you the way you want or need to be loved.

Forgiving strangers and friends is easier than forgiving family, but the process is the same, and it was just as powerful in moving my life forward.

As one of my favorite pastors, Joel Osteen, once said, "Some people you just have to love from a distance. Sometimes they're family. You see them once or twice a year and say, 'I love you,' but their negative attitude doesn't infiltrate your life."

I take Suzanne Somers's simple but powerful words to heart: "Forgiveness is a gift you give yourself." Now, each time I'm offended or hurt by anyone, I choose the path of giving myself the gift of forgiveness. After all, we live in a fallen human world with flawed people, and I'm immensely flawed. I want forgiveness when I mess up, so my heart is set to give the same.

4) Be willing to face that mirror daily.

In the book *Can't Hurt Me*, New York Times best seller and Navy SEAL David Goggins wrote, "Tell yourself the truth! That you've wasted enough time, and that you have other dreams that will take courage to realize. Call yourself out! Tell the truth about the real reasons for your limitations and you will turn that negativity which is real, into jet fuel. The odds against you will become a massive runway!"

He also refers to the act of dealing with self as the "accountability mirror." This is the central point of my entire life. I could blame others for my actions and point the finger to this person or that period, but in the end, the buck stops with me. If we're not moving forward in life or breaking barriers or obstacles, the first place to look is in the mirror.

For me, accountability has been deeply rooted in looking at myself and what I need to do in order to change, especially before I try to change others. The fact is I can't change anyone; I can only change me. When a blowup, issue, or challenge arises, or I find myself stuck, I ask myself three questions:

1) Why am I here? (Evaluate the factors that got me here.)

2) What did I contribute to the situation? (Own it, own it, own it.)

3) What can I do to change it? (Even if there are extenuating factors outside of my control, what can I do to make it better?) Then I take action and correct, leaving things outside of my control up to God.

Accountability must start with each of us! In my marriage and with my family, I have chosen to live my life by facing my accountability mirror. When stuff blows up in our lives, I take a step back and ask these questions. Then, instead of arguing my point until the cows come home, I try to rest, recalibrate, and renew my thought process around that issue or circumstance. It does no good to try to prove your point or be right all the time. A bit of humility and accountability goes a long way toward resolving problems.

When I realize I can't change or control anything or anyone, I make sure that the change starts with ME.

5) Release Control.

I'm a type A personality—someone who likes to drive, whether it be decisions, outcomes, or solutions. But often, those of us who like to drive also need to understand that when we can't drive, we should take a step back and just be still.

My executive coach, Jan, has worked with me over the years to help me recenter my thought process around issues that are outside of my control. Here are the three things I do to make this concept work for me in both my personal and professional life:

1) **Recognize** those things that *are* in my control and change them. For those things outside of my control, I mentally (and in my journal) put them in buckets, far enough away so I don't obsess about them, but close enough so I know what I'm dealing with.
2) **Sit and wait** for those things I can't control. Let them sit without taking action on them right away. Usually, if we step away from something that's blowing up or going bad and we allow ourselves to sit and be still, we'll find we can deal with it in a vastly different way the next day.
3) **Quiet your mind and thoughts** for three to five minutes every morning. I learned this strategy over the last few years. As a person who frequently has all things hitting her at once, quieting my mind each morning is essential to my success. I need my time of meditation, which includes reading

encouragement from God's Word or a devotional. Otherwise, my day goes awry.

In addition, the famous Serenity Prayer has provided me with a humbling perspective: "God grant me serenity to accept the things I cannot be change, courage to change the things I can, and wisdom to know the difference." I've centered the last three decades of my life around these words.

6) Adopt a lifestyle of continual learning and expansion.

Sometimes in life we want to settle for the cards we were dealt, settle for a passionless job, settle for mediocrity, settle for how we live, settle because we've been told it's just the way it is. I believe in getting outside of my comfort zone to push myself in areas where I'm uncomfortable until I get comfortable. If we don't ever push our boundaries in life, we won't experience anything different than where we are. In the Maxwell Leadership Bible, one of my favorite study Bibles, John Maxwell states three key areas of continual growth and learning:

1) "If you forget the ultimate, you will become a slave to the immediate." (Never lose sight of your goal.)
2) "Activity does not always mean accomplishment." (You can be busy, but it doesn't necessarily mean it has a good outcome or result.)
3) If I don't evaluate, I will become stagnant in life. (Continue to evaluate your growth.)

In summation, my journey has been a continual adoption of a lifestyle of five *R*s:

1) **Relearning**—Never stop learning.
2) **Reengineering**—Live in an attitude of reengineering, or redesigning.
3) **Rethinking**—Adopt an attitude of new thoughts and positive thinking.
4) **Reshaping**—Be willing to be flexible, even when it's uncomfortable.
5) **Renewing**—Recalibrate and renew yourself.

Be teachable. It's an important skill in your journey and on your path to fulfilling your purpose.

7) Never give up. Never relent. STAY the course.

Nothing happens overnight. Every good outcome in life requires a process, time, and a commitment to stay consistent. I recall a senior manager in my career who, around twenty years ago, described me from his perspective. He said, "When Rebecca hits a brick wall, she'll do one of two things: either she'll find a way around it, or she'll knock it down."

Why am I like that? Because there's no giving up.

However, before we start knocking down walls or circumventing them, it's important to evaluate *why* the brick wall is there. It may just be that the timing isn't right, and that wall is there to protect you. But if the timing is right, find a way around it or get a sledgehammer to bring it down. You need to stay the course with a consistent commitment to your goals, vision, and cause.

It's all too easy to give up, especially when we see so much negativity around us in the media, in what's happening in America and in the world. But we simply can't allow what we see or experience to distract us or derail us from our dreams or goals.

Keep in mind, throughout my journey and life, every single obstacle was stacked against me early on, including:

- poverty
- lack of motivation
- teen pregnancy
- dropping out of high school
- unstable home life
- no father figure
- addictions
- dysfunction
- mental trauma
- emotional trauma
- learning issues in school
- lack of higher education
- bad behaviors

The list goes on and on and could fill up this entire page.

However, staying the course in my transformative journey and holding on to the desire for more in life kept me from veering off the path of my purpose. It was determination. It was grit. Travis Bradberry put both into perspective when he said, "Grit is that 'extra something' that separates most successful people from the rest. It's the passion, perseverance, and stamina that we must channel in order to stick with our dreams until they become a reality."

Even now in my success, every January I make a goals list. When I hit barriers early in the year or midway through, I go back to that list and reread it, sharpen it, meditate and pray over it, and then I begin to speak my goals to myself. I declare them over my life and speak them into the atmosphere. No one, and I mean no one can steer me away from the goals I want to achieve.

But should things happen I have no control over and I don't reach a goal, then I move on to celebrate the ones I do achieve. I don't sulk or pout about what I lost, but I celebrate the wins I *do* have, even the small ones. This helps me stay the course.

Lastly, if you have people in your life who don't allow you to dream or question your capacity to achieve results or grow beyond where you are today, my recommendation is to get new people in your life who believe in you. You define your life's journey by the people you surround yourself with.

Your core group of friends, business confidants, and influencers should do five things:

1) encourage you in your dreams
2) celebrate your wins with you (and you, in turn, with them)
3) be there for you thick and thin (not just at mountaintops)
4) love you just as you are but love you enough to share the truth with you on those critical areas for growth
5) be people you can look up to and aspire to be like

People can make or break you. Core relationships are important, and equally important is evaluating those relationships or influences regularly to ensure they align with your dream or goals. This is the last nugget.

I hope *Lost Girl* has been an encouragement to you. I hope you share it with those in your inner circle who you believe need the encouragement and the ability to dream again.

I'm thankful that I got to live this wonderful story. I'm thankful God has blessed me to be able to share it with you so that you too can be encouraged in your own personal journey, give yourself permission to dream big and set great goals, and then work hard to achieve them. I'm thankful that my story doesn't end here but continues forward in whatever path I am to undertake next.

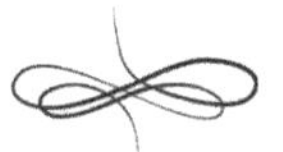

"'For I know the plans I have for you,' declares the LORD, 'plans to prosper you and not to harm you, plans to give you hope and a future.'"

—JEREMIAH 29:11 (NIV)

ABOUT THE AUTHOR: REBECCA CONTRERAS

Rebecca Contreras is currently the President & CEO of AvantGarde LLC (AG), a consulting firm she cofounded in 2011 as the majority owner. AG offers a one-stop-shop approach to addressing complex organizational, people, and technological needs. It has locations in both Texas and Washington DC, and Rebecca commutes between the two. To learn more about AG, visit www.avantgarde4usa.com.

Prior to moving into the consulting business, Rebecca spent fifteen years working in government. While living in DC, Rebecca served first as a Commissioned Officer to President George W. Bush in the Bush White House administration, managing the personnel appointments process for over 1,200 positions in the federal government. Then the president appointed her to lead corporate HR in the role of Deputy Assistant Secretary & Chief of Human Capital for the U.S. Department of Treasury, a workforce of 128,000 employees. Rebecca started her government career working as a civil servant for eleven years in Austin in Texas Government, including serving as the Director of Human Resources for the Office of Governor Bush for six years. Prior to joining the Governor's Office, she served six years at the State Treasury for female Texas icons Ann Richards and then Kay Bailey Hutchison.

In 2021, AG received the coveted Stevie Silver Award for Minority-Owned Business of the Year (American Business Awards). She also received numerous awards in 2020, including two global awards—Women in Enterprise by *Women Enterprising Magazine* and Women 2 Watch for 2020 by the Women President's Organization in New York City. Her company was also recognized during National Small Business Week with Texas District Award for Women Small Business of the Year and Federal Contractor Minority Business of the Year. Rebecca also received the Texas Women Profiles in Power award by the *Austin Business Journal*, and Governor Greg Abbott, in conjunction with the Texas Small Business Summit, also honored Rebecca with the Texas Latina Entrepreneurial Excellence Award.

Rebecca is also the cofounder with her husband, David, of LaunchPad, a nonprofit foundation that supports programs for inner-city families and underprivileged youth and causes in her hometown in Austin, Texas.

To learn more about Rebecca, visit her website at www.rebeccacontreras.com and follow her on Facebook or Instagram: @rebeccaanncontreras.